Celestial Gifts
Book Series

Angelic Symbols

Angelic Symbols of
the Purest Spiritual Healing Energy
and the Highest Light and Love to
Completely Purify, Perfectly Enhance,
and Totally Enlighten
Your Life, Here and Now

Georgios Mylonas
GEOM!*

Important Note

The recommendations made in this book should not be considered a replacement for formal medical or mental treatment. A physician should be consulted in all matters relating to health, including any symptoms that require medical attention. Anyone who has emotional, mental, or physical problems should seek professional consultation before attempting any of these practices. While the information and the suggestions in this book are believed to be safe and accurate, the author cannot accept liability for any harm as a result of the use or misuse of these practices. This book is intended as general information and for educational purposes.

First English edition 2015
© Georgios Mylonas
All rights reserved.
No part of this publication may be reproduced or transmitted in any form or by any means, electronic or mechanical, including photocopying, recording, or by any information storage and retrieval system, without the written permission of the publisher.
Copyright © 2010 by Georgios Mylonas

GEOM!*
Georgios Mylonas
Teacher and author on methods of energy healing,
personal development, and spiritual advancement

The School of Reiki, Athens
www.energiesoflight.com
www.universityofreiki.com
www.reiki.gr
e-mail: reiki@reiki.gr

Translated by Katerina Mantzaridou
Appendix Translated by Anastasia Christidou

ISBN: 9608960649
ISBN 13: 9789608960640

Ten percent of the proceeds from this book go to charity.

DEDICATION

This work is wholeheartedly dedicated to the healing, illumination,
and enlightenment of all beings and to their greatest and highest good.
It is a work from Love, to Love, through Love, and with Love.
It is therefore also dedicated to Love: the Unlimited, Boundless, Infinite Love;
the Alpha-Omega Love; the Angelic Love, and the Divine Love.

WISHES AND BLESSINGS

The book you now behold delivers great gifts, spiritual esoteric healing keys into
your hands. May it lead your mind to a higher sun and your heart to a new season
of spring. May this book lead your everyday self to wisdom, your physical body to
happiness, and your life to ecstatic wholeness, freedom, and fulfillment. We wish
infinite goods to all people, infinite goods to every single one of you, all the good
things that you—you, being right here, right now—divinely deserve!

ACKNOWLEDGMENTS

We wish to thank all those people who were directly or indirectly involved in the
creation of this book, but above all, we thank Spirit and its innumerable powers,
countless like the stars. We would like to thank Spirit for all the amazing, exquisite,
and sublime abilities of healing, self-discovery, and enlightenment that it offers to
humanity. They are some of the most wonderful proofs of the spiritual truth that "God
is Love." These are proofs of Spirit with which every human being can get acquainted
and, most essentially and most importantly, directly experience on the most intimate,
personal level.

With Divine Love,
the Angels of Pure Light

How to proceed with this work

The book that you now hold in your hands will lead you on an extraordinary—probably ecstatic—journey of self-discovery, self-healing, illumination, and enlightenment, as well as collective planetary healing and enlightenment, since the part affects the whole. It is a journey beyond imagination and expectation. You may not yet be fully aware of how many wondrous powers a human being hides inside him...in his heart, his soul, his spirit, or in his mind, this perfect instrument of consciousness. You may not yet be fully aware of the infinite wonders, the miracles the universe conceals—the enormous universe, the external just like the small universe-inside-the-universe, that inner universe of human existence. Are you prepared?

Initiate and embrace this journey with an open and pure mind; with an open and warm heart; with faith, trust, and love! These three powers make the world move; they birth and create the world. It is about a leap—a huge leap of consciousness beyond and above what is already known and familiar, beyond and above what is visible and apparent. It is a leap to the unknown. Engage in it with faith, trust, and love, and bear in mind that only good can come out of it—the Highest Good! You will see what can be seen only from the big picture, the great prism, a superior level of existence and awareness— the deepest, broadest, and most elevated level. It is a level of existence and awareness more macrocosmic, more hypercosmic—a level that, when we finally experience it, we exclaim, "Yes, this is how it should be done. In the end, everything was for good. It was all for the best!"

Contents

Introduction: *Celestial Gifts*

In a period of deep and intense spiritual work, I "heard" with my internal senses—the senses of the soul and spirit—the Angels saying that some small angelic books would be written, several heavenly gifts comprising one collective work. Each would be a different, parallel, and complementary path to come closer to the Angels and receive their help and support, their knowledge, their wisdom, and their love, to heal and improve— as much as it is possible and as much as we desire—our life on Earth.

These books would be called Celestial Gifts, and they were very soon ready and written in mind and spirit. They were put on paper in a short period of continuous inspiration and nonstop automatic writing, with no second thought, hesitation, judgment, or difficulty. A smooth flow of words coming straight from the heart and soul was all it took—just like the Angels would want it to happen, Angelically.

The material of Celestial Gifts includes positive affirmations and healing decrees; symbols of energy and spirit; secrets, tips, and techniques of spiritual connection and manifestation; energy invocations and prayers; Angelic meditations; and creative visualizations. These are keys and tools to inspire, guide, help, and support a person in his personal and collective path—beautiful and open gates of light, bridges of heavenly light! The Angels have given their assurance and proof that this is so—angelic assurance and angelic proof. But you now take on the most important proof of all: the proof of personal experience. To believe, experience! Experience to believe!

Enjoy these beautiful and luminous spiritual tools and keys, the gifts of Heaven. Celebrate with your entire being! Improve your life, and make it more radiant and illuminating, starting today...starting now! See the Light of Love and the Love of Light rising again within your beingness, rising to new crystal clear heights.

With Infinite Joy, Infinite Gratitude, and Infinite Love!
Infinitely Infinite.

The Angels

Take a deep, deep breath. One more...and another one...great!

Let's start from the beginning. What are the angels? Are they real? Do they really exist? Where are they? Do they ever appear in our lives, and if so, when? How can they help us? And how can we get closer to them?

The angels are immaterial light creatures, heavenly spiritual beings, real and existent in another dimension, on the higher levels of the Greater Reality. They reside in a higher, more expansive, more total, and more complete reality: a dimension of pure Beingness, the dimension of pure Spirit -a dimension of supreme and perfect peace, harmony, and love. The angels are heavenly messengers, just as the word *angel* denotes, deriving from the Greek word *angelos*, which means "messenger." They are messengers sent by God, messengers of the highest, supreme, and ultimate source, principle, and power, messengers of the divine source of all, of everything, of all things, visible and invisible, material and immaterial, known and unknown.

Their work is to transfer messages and energies from heaven to the earth, from the spiritual dimension to the material one, from the inner worlds to the external one. They connect the higher dimensions and planes of infinite Divine Beingness and transcendental pure Spirit to the dimension and plane of the earth and humanity. They transfer messages and energies from the level and realm of the supreme substance and essence to the level and realm of dense matter and manifestation; from the absolute unity and oneness, to the world of separation, opposites, and conflict.

The angels transfer messages and manifest energies from the inner planes to the outer, from the higher levels to the lower, from the spiritual planes to the material, and from the ultimate reality to the world of appearances, in this way bridging, connecting, coordinating, and aligning them. They constitute living bridges and living gates of ascension, enlightenment, and *theosis*—unification with the divine. They are bright bridges and luminous gates to higher freedom, peace, and blissfulness and sublime, complete, and total happiness. There are innumerable and countless angels, all of them most wonderful and admirable: messengers and bringers of unity and oneness, of peace and harmony, of tranquility and freedom, of wisdom and power, and of light and love. They are messengers and bringers of the greatest, the highest, the supreme, the eternal, the infinite, the divine essence of spirit: Love. Love and beauty lie everywhere and in everything! There is so much beauty and love in the cosmos, in the universe, on Earth, and in nature, but there is even more beauty and love deeper within and higher above!

The angels are pure, all-pure beings; they are pure, radiant consciousnesses that serve the Divine Plan and the Divine Purpose, serving the order, the harmony, the evolution, and the perfectness of the Highest Plan and Purpose. They aid in the manifestation of this Plan. They help in the fulfillment of this Purpose. It is a Plan of Supreme Light and Love and a Purpose of Ultimate Love and Light. It is a transcendental, concealed, mysterious, and mystical plan and purpose. This plan and purpose are incomprehensible and inconceivable to the human mind as they expand through eternity and infinity, through divinity itself.

There are innumerable and countless angels and groups of angels. The angels transcend religions. They have existed long before them, long before humankind. They have existed long before anything since the Creation and probably the beginning of Beingness. Nobody really knows for sure. They emanate from the Transcendental, Unknown, and Most-High Divine Source, Dimension, and Beingness, from the Supreme and Absolute Reality; they are far and above all manifestations and worldly phenomena and commune in the Divine Perfection, Wholeness, Blissfulness, and Oneness.

We can say that the angels are the "hands" of God, of Divine Beingness. They are the "reflections" or "thoughts" of God, of the Divine. They are Divine "thoughts"! We can picture them as sun rays assuming that the sun represents the Infinite and Absolute Divine Beingness, the Supreme Divine Reality, what we call "the Most High" or, alternatively, "the Highest Reality," a level behind, above, and beyond all worldly phenomena. The angels are bright rays, luminous existences, and illuminating divine reflections. They are living, radiant rays of power, wisdom, and love of the one supreme sun, the cosmic sun, the hyper-, super-, and ultra cosmic sun, the greatest sun of all time and space, of all of creation and of all universes, of all levels, planes, dimensions, and realities. A sun—a divine field inside everything and extending behind, above, and beyond everything. Can we imagine this? Or at least, can we start imagining it?

The angels are found—as conceptual ideals and as real, existent beings—so far away yet so close. They are unapproachable yet approachable. Invisible and immaterial yet so visible and material. So unknown and yet so familiar. So mysterious, hidden, and mystical yet so cordial, friendly, and loving. They constitute the ideal, the higher aspect of humanity, even though they possess a separate existence on their own. They are humanity dreaming of itself with wings—wings of freedom, power, and happiness. But keep in mind that this ideal exists regardless of humanity. It is not that humanity dreams of something that is inexistent; it dreams of something that exists and that always existed—it existed before humanity itself. Now, this ideal embraces humanity with its higher consciousness, energy, and love. How could something lower ever dream of something that is higher? The higher preexists and is immanent in the "lower," and when the lower is ready, the higher is awakened, and it reaches down to it. It finally touches and embraces the lower, elevating, healing, and illuminating it, taking it to ever-higher states.

The angels embody, express, and manifest a great variety of spiritual and energetic qualities, characteristics, and powers. They can guide, direct, protect, heal, purify, attract, reveal, create, and bring forth any element of life, anything that we can possibly need. In essence, the angels constitute the manifestation of the Absolute Divine Beingness; they are the Absolute Divine Beingness in Action. Expressing Itself. Vibrating. Radiating. They are the Supreme Divine Consciousness (the highest and absolute consciousness of All That Is) in action, God manifested, and the Fiery Love of the Divine for Its Creation and for humanity in full and perfect expression, communication, and revelation. The angels express, communicate, and reveal the Will of the Highest Reality and Source; of the Infinite, the Eternal, the Absolute, the Divine.

In fact, angels constitute incarnations of God, aspects and facets of God, or, with greater accuracy, facets and aspects of the different qualities of God. They form His infinite qualities and energies. Consequently, there are angels of healing, nature, grace, mercy, power, knowledge, and wisdom, as well as angels of romance, family, friendship, love, and forgiveness. There are angels of health, vitality, protection, guidance, and abundance, as well as angels of thoughts, emotions, relationships, spiritual development, enlightenment, and ascension. Angels of fire, water, and air, as well as of ether and matter. Angels of beauty, harmony, and music, as well as of colors, arts, and sciences. Angels of plants and crystals and of the stars and celestial phenomena, as well as of universal laws. Qualities, characteristics, and properties that man himself already possesses—whether they are expressed and manifested or they are waiting as possibilities—are immanent and inherent in his being as he is created in God's own image, a mirror of the Divine. These are qualities, characteristics, and properties that he has the ability to discover and develop in himself by receiving experiences, lessons, and knowledge related to them—experiences, lessons, and knowledge of the self, of the world, of life, and of the Divine.

There are reports regarding angels in most spiritual traditions, eras, and religions: pagan and monotheistic, eastern and western, ancient and contemporary. Nevertheless, the angels call us to go far and beyond the doctrines and beliefs so that we sense and experience on a personal level, in our own personal truths, their presence and existence, their properties and characteristics, and their energies and vibrations, as well as their love and power. These constitute major and deep existential experiences of the soul and the spirit (even of our physical bodies) that prove—once and for all—the higher and greater existence and reality and the innermost meaning and value of All That Is. The harmony and perfection of all. The true, real, transcendental, ecstatic divinity of all. Unconditional divinity, unlimited divinity! Alpha-Omega Divinity.

The angels send us their pure love and wish us to meet them with an open mind, open heart, open spirit, open hands, and open arms. They want us to meet them with a smile and laughter, awareness and responsibility, courage and awe, childlikeness and innocence. They want us to meet them inside our minds and hearts, inside others, inside life, nature, and the universe. They want us to meet them high above, at the top of the existence. Here, where peace, tranquility, harmony, love, and perfection eternally vibrate and flourish, ecstatically, in their never-ending blissfulness.

Blessings, angelic blessings!

Twenty-One Fundamental Facts about the Angels

1. Angels are immaterial spiritual beings, meaning that they consist of spirit and not matter. They consist of light and energy.

2. They are bodiless.

3. They are immortal spirits.

4. They aren't limited by matter.

5. They are not limited by space and time.

6. Their number cannot be estimated; it is uncountable.

7. They are perpetually moving.

8. They don't belong to a particular sex.

9. They have distinctive qualities.

10. They serve God (the Highest Reality and Source of All).

11. They were created by divine, ecstatic love.

12. They constitute manifestations of the Divine.

13. They were created so that the Divine can share and manifest its divine, ecstatic love.

14. They are everywhere.

15. They travel like thoughts do.

16. They constitute bridges toward the Divine Consciousness.

17. They represent, form, and manifest Divine Properties and Qualities.

18. They possess all the knowledge and powers of the universe.

19. They mediate between Spirit and matter, man and the Divine.

20. They guide and support the development and evolution of man, his return to supreme consciousness, existential wholeness and oneness.

21. They are God's living gift to man.

Being Closer to the Angels

Under what conditions and circumstances are we closer to the angels, these pure, spiritual, heavenly beings?

We are closer to the angels in the following situations:

- when we relax, pray, or meditate
- when we have high energy levels
- when we are close to nature
- when we sleep
- when we are in alternative levels-states-waves of consciousness, beyond our daily alertness
- when we experience ecstasy or intense euphoria
- when we keep our minds open
- when we become more spiritually sensitive or aware
- when we follow our intuition
- when we are in areas and places of great energy power
- when we are in temples
- when we receive a spiritual or healing attunement, empowerment, or initiation
- when we give or receive energy or spiritual healing
- when we daydream
- when we are overwhelmed by happiness, love, or romance
- when we have clarity
- when we simply think of angels
- when we are at crucial points in our lives or in despair, danger, or intense pain— physical or emotional
- when we are about to receive some higher message or inner guidance
- when we have requested it
- when someone has requested it with great love on our behalf

Angelic Signs

What are the signs and indications of the angels in our lives? The angels are trying to make their presence perceptible, to communicate with us, to guide us, or to lead us toward our healing and spiritual development in numerous ways, and mainly as follows:

- when we see lights, rays of light, spheres of light, smoke, clouds, or even forms in our space
- when we see them before we sleep, or when we wake up
- when we see them in a state of relaxation and daydreaming
- when we listen to a report about angels on the radio or on TV
- when we read something relevant about them in a magazine or a book
- when a message comes to us as an answer to our queries
- when we open randomly a book and come across the answer to our query
- when we meet a person who, with his/her words, provides the answer to our questions, or confirms our thoughts
- when we find a peculiar feather in the street or a white feather
- when we come across a special object that we sense has been laid there by the angels or that was sent by "those above"
- when a problem of ours finds its solution miraculously or inexplicably
- when we sense intense heat, numbness, or a tingle in our body
- when we sense drafts of air and shiver
- when we feel deeply emotional
- when we feel as if we are immobilized
- when we feel unprecedented clarity and lucidity
- when we experience euphoria, happiness, peace, gratitude, or a sense of security
- when we have high inspiration
- when we sense "company" in our space—a feeling that we are not alone

All of the above are indications that angels are close to us, even by our side, enfolding and embracing us with their guiding light and healing love.

How to Consciously Connect to Angels

There are some quite simple ways to easily recognize and identify the pure spiritual energies of the angels in your life and experience more of their magnificent blessings and absolute positivity.

* Open your heart. Bring to your attention the energy center of the heart, found in the middle of the chest, at least once a day, and visualize there a beautiful blooming flower. It is a very simple but highly transforming exercise. Perform it daily. Feel the openness and love.

* Become children—children in the heart, filled with the joy of exploration and discovery. See the world from a new perspective—in curiosity and admiration. Don't take everything for granted! Discover everything from the beginning! Children hold the keys to Life.

* Purify your energy, thoughts, and emotions. Purify yourself from all unwanted, unnecessary, heavy, and painful emotions, as well as negative thoughts. Seek for practical and effective ways to achieve that.

* Discover the hidden purity and innocence of your deeper, real self. Return to that. It is always there, inside us.

* Think of the angels. Bring them to mind as often as you can.

* Feel them. Feel their energy. Practice. Be patient and insistent. Become more sensitive. Open yourself up to higher, more subtle sensations.

* Distinguish their energy. How do you feel when it is close?

* Invoke them. Ask for their presence.

* Pray. Prayer elevates your energy levels. Pray genuinely and authentically, from your heart and with your whole being. Pray with total faith and love.

* Send the angels love and gratitude; thank them from your deep within your heart.

* Use the Angelic Symbols. Study the Angelic Symbols. Feel them, meditate on them, and apply them. Add them to your daily life in many ways.

* Use energy and spiritual techniques. Discover the ones that you like best, and perform them on a daily basis.

* Light a white candle. Dedicate it while you are lightening it. Gaze at its warm, golden flame for a while and relax. Feel its flame, embracing you with its fiery energy. It is the pure warm light of Spirit that purifies your mind and aura.

* Reflect on them before you sleep. Perform a brief meditation, an invocation, or a prayer. Invoke them with love and anticipation. Feel safety and warmth.

* Pay attention to your dreams. Notice them and observe them. Record them and analyze them intuitively, according to your inner guidance, or simply record them without any mental analysis.

* Keep an angelic diary with reflections, meditations, symbols, invocations, dreams, experiences, thoughts, and personal events, as well as poems, inspirations, and your own plans. Dedicate this diary to the angels by simply holding it in your hands and affirming your dedication.

* Dedicate your house to the Highest Angels! Do it out loud, and visualize them guarding it inside the Divine Light. Invoke them daily!

* Perform a good deed every day—a good, altruistic deed—with appreciation, purity, and love. Do it spontaneously and genuinely. Live a day to offer and eventually a life of offer. Create good karma!

* Treat everyone with love—higher love. This applies even to animals and plants.

* Speak with nice words. Speak with words of acceptance, love, and support toward everyone and everything. Make sure that your speech is positive and bright. Speak positively and brightly.

* Become aware of the Divine element. Recognize it inside you and inside all others.

* Ask for guidance from the angels—on any issue. Don't worry that you may deprive them of their time because they seek for opportunities to manifest divine healing energies on Earth.

* Let your imagination, your awareness, and your senses roam entirely free. Why should they only function partly? Declare that the totality of your mind functions at 100 percent. State it several times during the day. Notice the difference.

* Recognize the signs! Become observant! Be hyper- and ultra observant.

* Come into contact with nature. Come closer to Mother Nature; relax deeply and rest completely close to her. Respect her, take care of her, and be aware of her wonders to the fullest extent. Feel the love, unity, serenity, and harmony that are overabundant in Mother Nature. Pure perfection.

* Visit areas and places of special energetic vibration and importance: ancient and contemporary temples and other places of spiritual and vital power.

* Meditate. Close your eyes, take deep breaths, relax, and observe your breath and energy.

* Practice visualization. Relax completely, and let your consciousness, awareness, and imagination totally free. Visualize that you are under a waterfall of pure, bright, vital light. See and feel the light as much as possible surrounding you, permeating you, and filling you with its warm luminosity. See and feel yourself healthy and happy, pure and radiant, and full of love and wisdom. Then see and feel yourself connecting on an energy level with your guardian angel or the archangels. Call them with

love and gratitude, feel their presence, and talk to them. Communicate with them mentally, spiritually, and from the heart. Remain in their high angelic love, light, and energy for some time. For optimal benefits and results, practice this on a daily basis.

* Clear away your fear: send it away, once and for all. Fear is the exact opposite of love! It is the opposing energy, the opposing state of consciousness. Remove, cancel, and banish the fear completely out of your inner being. It is a dense wall of selfishness and false security, an energetic, mental, and emotional wall in front of your spiritual good, your highest good, which is love—all love and only love.

* Fill yourself with gratitude! Gratitude is a heavenly state and an angelic quality. Feel and experience gratitude, which is real, deep thankfulness toward everyone and everything, toward the whole of existence. Make a list of all things for which you are grateful.

* Surrender yourself to awe. Feel awe for the cosmos, the universe, and existence. For Life and consciousness. Ask yourself and wonder! Feel the greatness, the infiniteness, the miracle. Then, just immerse yourself in total awe!

All of the above-mentioned simple and easy methods will open up, align, and connect you to the angels on a deeper level and help you form a strong relationship with them so that you personally and directly experience all of their truly beneficial qualities and healing characteristics.

How Angels Can Help You

What can angels offer us? Why should we connect with them and call them in our lives? By consciously calling and openly welcoming the angels in your life, many benefits, blessings, and positive results follow. Here are some of these:

- You connect to the Divine Itself.
- You call forth and recognize the Divine element in your daily life.
- You fill your life with spiritual light, pure energy, and vital energy.
- You fill yourself with love—unconditional, unlimited, heavenly, angelic love.
- You feel more power and support.
- You experience higher safety and protection.
- You receive increased guidance and direction.
- You receive answers to your queries.
- You connect with your core—the essence of your existence, your spirit, and your soul.
- You understand yourself more and more and the reasons why things happen.
- You discover meaning and purpose.
- You awaken your mental and spiritual powers and your intuition and vision.
- You awaken the abilities of spiritual healing and self-healing that you possess.
- You help more people.
- You align to universal prosperity and go with the flow of life.
- You become a channel of light.
- You ground your higher self. You manifest it in the present in your daily life.
- You acquire higher knowledge and wisdom.
- You become a fully conscious member of your greater spiritual family.
- You bond with your most loving spiritual siblings, companions, and friends; that's what the angels are to you.
- You learn to love more truthfully and purely.
- You learn to transcend the impediments and hardships
- You perceive everything that goes on around you as spiritual challenges that offer lessons and great knowledge; these challenges hide valuable gifts.

- You participate actively in the heavenly plan—the universal and cosmic plan of light and love.
- You help the planet in its process of healing, evolution, and enlightenment.
- You become a source of higher light and love for everyone and everything.
- You become what you are meant to be: an angel on Earth.

The Angelic Symbols

The Angelic Symbols are spiritual symbols of higher energy, pure light, and pure love. They are special energy tools that focus spiritual vital energy. They are keys to specific qualities and properties, from the infinite Spectrum of Light, Spirit, and Life. The Angelic Symbols are means of and keys to focus and concentration: they focus and concentrate the mind, the powers and qualities of the higher mind, and our intentions; they help us express more of our total power and complete potential. They have the effect and power that we attribute to them, but at the same time they possess power of their own, by themselves, due to their archetypical form and the intention that created and activated them.

Independently and beyond our own beliefs, the Angelic Symbols radiate and transmit a unique aura and specific energy characteristics because their nature and essence are transcendental. They inherently possess inner functions and specific frequencies that transcend the human factor. That means that they have power, energy, influence, and activity that are irrelevant to whether we believe in them or to whether we understand them through reason. They resemble the water that washes you out, whether you believe in it or not, whether you understand how and why this happens or not. This becomes even more evident while we study and experiment on them as we notice different sensations, distinct energies, and specific qualities in each one of them, without being fully aware of how they function or even what they represent and symbolize. When we energetically draw them on other people, they perceive and confirm that something is happening indeed!

The Angelic Symbols are spiritual symbols with pure, bright, and vital energy attributes and have been sent through higher spiritual guidance and inspiration. Their aim is total healing, holistic healing; they are therapy and balance for all levels of being: the physical body, the energy system, the psyche, the mind, and the spirit. Their context is personal and collective evolution, advancement, and betterment. Their base is the good, the higher good of all. Personal, collective, and planetary good. They have been created, activated, and exclusively offered for the good of all—the highest good. On this basis and within this context, they are completely and absolutely positive and benefi-cial: hyper bright and ultra luminous. They bring us closer to our own good; our highest good; and the spiritual, essential, true, and real good. It is the plan of the greatest light and the highest love. It is the celestial and cosmic plan, the Divine Plan, the plan for mankind. It is a perfect plan that includes everything that exists—us and the angels, these magnificent, exquisite, heavenly creatures that support and help man in his spiri-tual and earthly journey.

The Symbols are an instrument and a means of guidance, support, and facilitation of the spiritual and earthly journey of Life, serving the same purpose of all other symbols, like those of language, written speech, math, music, arts, and even technology. The Angelic Symbols comprise condensed or codified spiritual energies and spiritual angelic proper-ties. We can think of the Angelic Symbols as pure angelic energies and spiritual qualities in the form of symbols. They are angelic projections, entities, or forms: "angelics."

The Angelic Symbols constitute a complete system of high consciousness for the illu-mination and enlightenment of the mind and the energy system of man, of our entire field, which encompasses all of our thoughts and emotions, from the conscious outer to the deepest and most unconscious levels, the aura and the chakras (the energy centers of the body), and even our physical-material-biological body. The spiritual and energy healing symbols—and in this specific case, the Angelic Symbols—function primarily in the consciousness and energy level of our being, affecting and benefiting as a result all levels of the self and all areas of life, as it is a known truth that everything is conscious-ness; all is energy.

They have the ability to illuminate, enlighten, purify, motivate, inspire, elevate, release, harmonize, activate, and bring about greater states of happiness, peace, and wholeness. They light up our primary nature, whose essence is of divine origin and supreme Divine Light and Love. We can use the Angelic Symbols with trust and love, with respect and gratitude, without fear and limitations. They are an angelic gift, a most pure, power-ful, and truly healing gift! Heavenly gift! Gift of life, light, and love! Universal, cosmic, heavenly gift! Gift of the source, a divine gift! It is a gift that we ourselves requested, a gift that we ourselves longed for. A gift that we ourselves, on another level, along with the highest angels of the highest light, created and sent, out of love and mercy, out of recognition and praise to our earthly, incarnated self!

Only good can come out of their usage. Unlimited, infinite, unconditional good to all!

Characteristics and Properties of the Angelic Symbols

The Angelic Symbols constitute a spiritual energy code of communication—an angelic language. It is a language of light, healing, empowerment, peace, serenity, freedom, and love. The Angelic Symbols constitute a gift of heaven to earth, a gift of the angels to man. They spring from a higher level of consciousness and have been received, created, and activated through a deep, meditative process. They have been offered as an answer to a particular request of the writer that concerns the healing and advancement of all people. Like in all issues, "Ask and it is given" applies in this case under the condition that man is ready and willing to do what it takes (to offer his own part and dedicated work) so as to receive.

The Angelic Symbols are absolutely positive and entirely bright; they can't be used in a negative or in a wrong way or cause any harm. They have inherent energy-healing qualities and properties; they constitute codes of light that transfer, transmit, and channel pure, angelic energies. They possess their own intelligence and offer innumerable possibilities. They vibrate, are alive, and possess a form of consciousness. They connect with the angels, they represent them, and they align with angelic states and energies, manifesting them here and now. The angels themselves desire them to be given as a means of communication and manifestation. The angels themselves created them and activated them.

The symbols are very easy to use. They function and are immediate and effective. It is recommended that they be used with pure love and respect, with pure and positive intention, for the highest good of all. It is also recommended that they be used with humbleness and honesty and in the highest gratitude. Keep in mind that they are focused on the Highest Good and are derived from it. The Highest Good is their source and premise and their frame and context, and toward the Highest Good, they always guide and lead the way.

What the Angelic Symbols Offer

The Angelic Symbols do the following:

* They attract angels and angelic energies (divine qualities and properties) in our lives.
* They function holistically, meaning wholly. They exert their influence on all levels: they affect the consciousness and the energy and consequently the mind, the emotion, the aura, and the body (all is energy that vibrates on different levels).
* They act purely positively.
* They have a cleansing, purifying, healing, and invigorating effect.
* They support the spiritual development of man.
* They purify and reorganize the mind and the psyche (the emotional body).
* They act on the conscious, subconscious, and superconscious levels.
* They discharge all that is negative.
* They help us release the lower, limited, wounded self; our flaws; and our negative, dark, past, dense energies.
* They purify our auras and chakras, charging them with pure vitality.
* They manifest more light in our lives and the lives of the people around us.
* They provide energy and spiritual protection because they function as shields.
* They lead to abundance. Spiritual abundance is that of all levels and forms: holistic, substantial, true abundance.
* They elevate and uplift our consciousness.
* They connect us with the angelic kingdom and the higher realms of pure Spirit far and above the world of dense matter.
* They provide power and guidance.
* They give blessings.
* They light and enlighten.
* They bestow knowledge and wisdom.
* They awaken talents and abilities.
* They offer optimism, hope, faith, and trust.
* They activate the positive and bright side of ourselves—the beautiful, angelic side.

* They add beauty to our daily lives.
* They have a healing effect in situations and issues that worry us.
* They inspire and motivate.
* The simple images of the symbols elevate and activate the consciousness.
* The image of the symbols alone manifests vital and rejuvenating energy!
* They offer peace, serenity, joy, and euphoria, and they can even lead to ecstatic experiences, states of transcendent expansion, and oneness.
* They empower our spiritual and energy field. We become brighter.
* They unfold our spiritual intelligence.
* They lead toward greater self-knowledge. What we perceive around us we also discover within us and vice versa.
* They help us come into closer contact with ourselves, our needs, and our priorities.
* They attune us with the angels of heaven and help us in angelic communication and guidance.
* They activate inside us the angelic love, the divine love: the boundless, primary, and perfect love; love with no judgment and with no ego; love that is unconditional and unlimited. It is selfless love that heals everything and gives meaning, value, purpose, fulfillment, and happiness to the life of man.

The Angelic Symbols will probably act in a purifying and cleansing way, causing various symptoms that are temporary and transient and lead overall to a better and improved condition. Focus on staying extra positive, patient, peaceful, loving, attentive, observant, and aware!

Instructions for Use

Below are specific suggestions, advice, and some simple but essential rules so that you can begin your personal, spiritual work with the Angelic Symbols.

1. Start by making yourself more receptive. Become more sensitive, open your mind and spirit, and keep your heart wide open. The heart is your spiritual center, the center of enlightenment and love. It is the center of spiritual unity and true communication. Open yourself as much as you can, become totally sensitive, and place yourself in a state of absolute receptivity. Open yourself to the possibilities, the abilities, and the unknown with expectation and awe and without fear. Leave all fear and insecurity out. Feel the deepest awe and the greatest joy! Become like a child.

2. View all the Angelic Symbols meditatively. Read through the book slowly and steadily. Have a look at every symbol. The sight of a symbol, alone, activates, rejuvenates, and elevates the consciousness and energy levels. The symbols include archetypical structures. Approach them holding a mental stance of complete receptivity and total openness.

3. Observe them, internalize them, and feel them within you. What do you sense? How do you feel?

4. Choose the symbols that attract you: the symbols that you like, that impress you, or that you feel you need. Observe them for a while. Draw them on a piece of paper. Experiment with different colors. Draw the symbols that you have chosen several times. Draw every symbol with different colors. Practice it as a meditation. It is a high-energy exercise of connection with the symbols and their energies.

5. Visualize the symbols. See them mentally with the eyes of your mind. See them in your mind, gold and bright, radiating pure energy and golden light. Visualize them steadily. Keep them in your mind long enough and as much and as clearly as you

can. Visualization is the Alpha and Omega of spiritual co-creation. Practice it daily, even for a few minutes.

6. Draw and activate the symbols energetically, on the etheric level. Do this by drawing in the air the symbol or the symbols that you have chosen with your right hand, using your palm. Hold your right palm in the air in front of you, keeping it open outward (as if you are waving at someone), with the fingers joined together (as if you are slightly pushing against an invisible wall). Draw the symbol in front of you, in the air. It is as if you have paint on your palm and are drawing the symbol on an invisible canvas. Draw the symbol in the air in the same way that you would draw it on paper. Trace it with your hand movements, in front of you. You can draw it only with your fingers or with only one finger, but using the entire palm is more powerful. Draw it the way that you perceive it. There is no right or wrong in the means or the direction of drawing. Once you draw it, keep your palm in the air and feel the energy flowing, vibrating, and manifesting.

7. While you picture it in your mind or after you have drawn it with your hand in the air, say three or more times the name of the symbol or its property—for example, "Angelic Love, Angelic Love, Angelic Love," "Angelic Light, Angelic Light, Angelic Light," or "Archangel Michael, Archangel Michael, Archangel Michael." Say it mentally (inward) or out loud, but always slowly and steadily. Try to mean what you say. Understand it and stress the words as if you are manifesting them through the spoken word. Speak slowly and steadily, pointing out, meaning, expressing, and feeling what you say.

8. Once you have visualized or drawn in the air the symbol, and after you have said its name mentally or out loud three or more times, wait for a while and let yourself become more sensitive to its frequency, vibration, and energy. Make observations: What do you feel? How do you feel? Do you have any images or colors in your mind? Do you sense anything happening in you? If so, where? What is going on inside you? What is going on around you? What do you see and hear? Do you feel heat or cold, a sense of fire or air, flow or waves, electric or magnetic sensations, or vibrations, pulsing, tingling, or numbing? Become totally attentive. Do you have any feeling? Relax more and observe. Take your time. Repeat. Do it again. Repeat with the same symbol several times, and then experiment with other symbols as well. Become extra-attentive, observant, and sensitive to the various frequencies, vibrations, and specific energies of each symbol.

9. Devote some more time to every symbol. Perform each process slowly and meditatively. Relax even more. Place yourself in an even higher state of openness, receptivity, and sensitivity.

10. Once you begin your personal work with the symbols, you can use at any time the entirety of symbols in the order that they are given or randomly, or one symbol alone, or a combination of symbols that you need or that interest you. There are no strict rules or limitations. Experiment freely with one, with a combination, or with all the symbols.

11. Use your favorite symbols on a daily basis, as many times as you wish. Use them when you are in a state of relaxation, meditation, prayer, or invocation. You may also use them in a state of alertness, as you go through your daily routines. Use them alone or in a combination with other energy and spiritual methods and techniques. Use them as often as you wish.

12. Start and close your day with the Angelic Symbols.

13. Think about your favorite Angelic Symbol during the day.

14. Meditate on all the symbols, your favorite ones, or only on one symbol.

15. Use the Angelic Symbols to bless yourself and your life, your beloved ones, those who need light, or those who ask for your help and guidance. You can even bless the whole planet.

16. Have faith and trust. Work positively in a bright disposition. Once more, work with an open mind, open spirit, and open heart. Have angelic and divine openness.

17. Always listen to your inner voice and inner wisdom. Connect with your inner self, your inner being. There is infinite wisdom inside you. Connect with it, listen to it, and follow it. Use the Angelic Symbols intuitively, in your own way, and—above all—with love. Use them with the greatest love! The greater love you put into any work, the greater the love you receive!

18. Perceive the Angelic Symbols as angels guiding you to all relevant areas of life mani-

festing the corresponding pure energies and qualities. Respect them and honor them. Show gratitude and humility. Express your best and most wise self—the higher and most bright self. At the same time, express freely your potential without any limitation or fear.

19. Find out on your own more ways to use the Angelic Symbols, to express their essence and energy, to apply their light and love, and to experience the new paths and possibilities they provide.

Examples

   A. Draw your favorite symbol or the symbol that you need

      * on your notebook or agenda;

      * on a piece of paper (and place it on the wall, your altar, or your personal place of spiritual focus); or

      * on a piece of paper or an object (and give it to a person as a blessing).

   B. Energize and bless any space by placing papers (or objects) with Angelic Symbols on them in several spots of that space. In this way, you create a powerful field of pure angelic energy.

   C. Draw on a piece of paper an Angelic Symbol and put it under a glass or a bottle of water, leaving it there for a few hours to energize and activate the water. Then drink it by receiving its exquisite and higher vibration since the water is a receptive carrier of intentions, thoughts, emotions, and energies.

20. Always remember that the angels are divine beings, forms, and rays of spiritual energy, light, and love. Therefore, the Angelic Symbols are keys and codes of spiritual energy, light, and love. They constitute codes of communication with the angels, the angelic qualities, and their properties; they are also keys to ground and manifest all those high qualities and positive properties inside our beings and in our lives.

21. Finally, the symbols contribute to our happiness and the happiness of the people around us. They can offer abundant blessings, abundant energies, pure and beloved energies, and an abundance of spirit beyond every imagination and expectation. They can bring gifts of all sorts, including what man's heart and soul truly desire and all that is good, bright, beautiful, and true in the highest degree.

Below are frequently asked questions concerning the Angelic Symbols and the answers to them followed by the Angelic Symbols themselves. Make them part of your life now and experiment with them fearlessly, with an open mind, open spirit, and open heart. Be free to enjoy and love them. Love them with joy; enjoy them with love. Enjoy and love them with purity, awe, and a childlike spirit, and share them! Share them with the ones who desire to be benefited by these gifts.

Lovingly, work with the angels. Angelically, work with love.

Questions and Answers Regarding the Angelic Symbols

What are the Angelic Symbols?

The Angelic Symbols are spiritual keys with specific energy properties and energy characteristics. They broadcast and transmit high vibrations and high frequencies of Spirit.
They constitute key symbols for the manifestation of spiritual and pure qualities out of
the great energy realm of the light and the energies that promote healing and development on all levels. We can see them as gates of the earthly to the heavenly level and of
the celestial to the earthly level. We can perceive them as energy and light codes. They
function as bridges between the immaterial and the material, affecting positively all
phenomena. The Angelic Symbols bring the angels and their angelic energies closer to
us, serving the higher good, which is nothing other than the happiness and enlightenment of all.

How do the Angelic Symbols function?

The Angelic Symbols unlock qualities of universal vital energy (ethereal vitality, energy of life). They act as archetypes on the subconscious and as etheric prototypes that
are printed on the aura (the etheric field), purifying, lighting, and healing it. The aura
and the etheric field in their turn affect all levels because the etheric or energy body
contains and permeates the material or physical body. The Angelic Symbols have intelligence and consciousness of their own. They are transcendental and represent angelic
energies of great wisdom and love. They constitute a gift of heaven (the infinite spirit),
one of the many gifts that man and all beings, as divine essences, deserve.

How do I choose which Angelic Symbols to use?

You can choose Angelic Symbols in different ways. You can pick the symbols that attract you the most, either by their shape and form, or their name and function. You can also choose symbols that seem relevant and useful in order to cleanse, uplift, balance, empower, and illuminate an area of your life, and any issue or situation you want support with. Choose the symbols that you wish to work with, according to your needs or simply be free, choose intuitively and experiment. You may also simply open the book at random and pick symbols. Another way is to start at the beginning and work through the totality of the symbols, one by one, in the succession they are given, by practicing some symbols each day. In any case, you cannot choose the wrong symbols, as all symbols have a positive, bright, angelic impact on all levels, areas, and issues.

How can I use them?

You can simply look, observe, feel, and absorb them with your sight. Admire them and love them. Wonder and question. Reflect and meditate on them. You can connect with them on an energy level by drawing them on a piece of paper with a gold marker or with other colors, experimenting with the specific effects of different colors. You can also draw them in front of you in the air using your hand or fingers. Moreover, you can visualize them, seeing them with your mind's eye. Visualize them gold and bright like the sun, radiating their pure, golden energy and vital power. Do it daily and try to maintain your visualization long enough, as much as you can. The more you practice your visual abilities, the more effective your visualization becomes. Visualization calls for frequent practice. You can visualize the symbols in front of you, in the space, or inside you, such as in the heart chakra (the center of the chest) or in each of the seven chakras. Experiment with different symbols using all three ways—drawing them energetically with your hand in the air, visualizing them, or drawing them on a piece of paper using different colors—and observe the differences. For the best possible results, perform on a daily basis and experiment freely and abundantly!

Are there any additional ways to use them?

You can put a glass or a bottle of water on a piece of paper with an angelic symbol drawn on it. In this way, the angelic form and energy of the symbol is recorded in the water, which is the most receptive carrier of the energies of nature. Water is activated, programmed, and charged with vitality. Leave the water on the symbol for a few hours. There is no such thing as a specific time rule to follow. Work on it intuitively. You can do the same with anything else you desire to activate, program, and charge (e.g., a crystal or a charm). Moreover, you can draw with your palm or the fingers the symbol on the water or the object you wish to charge and visualize the symbol.

How can I energize and bless my space with the Angelic Symbols?

Energize the space by visualizing the symbols you desire in the space or by drawing the symbols with your palm or fingers in the air, sending them and infusing them (through your intention) on every wall and corner of the space. Furthermore, you can place pieces of white paper on which the Angelic Symbols are drawn with a golden color or with intense, bright colors. The Angelic Symbols protect and brighten the space energetically, transforming and elevating it. Anyone can sense the positive difference and the purity of energy within such an activated angelic space.

Can anyone use the Angelic Symbols?

Anyone can use them and receive their innumerable benefits. They are definitely safe, and they are as the angels: they bring nothing less than good!

How many times do I have to use them? Is there a specific plan that I should follow?

There are no rules or limitations, only suggestions. You can create your own plan of work depending on your needs and aims by following your inner guidance and intuition. As the symbols are used more and more and are studied more deeply, more specific programs and ways of using them will emerge in the future.

Where can the Angelic Symbols be of help to me?

First of all, the Angelic Symbols function and act on an etheric-energy level. In this way, they influence all levels: the body, the emotions, the mind, and the spirit. They cleanse, purify, balance, harmonize, elevate, empower, release, brighten, illuminate, and enlighten. They constitute a simple, practical, easy-to-use yet direct, powerful, and effective means of individual and collective healing, evolution, and growth toward the Highest Good of All, the happiness and enlightenment of all beings.

Can I show them freely to everyone? Must someone be initiated or attuned to them?

Anyone can come into contact with the Angelic Symbols. They require no previous knowledge or other capabilities, nor some specific form of learning or tutoring. The simple viewing and the use and application of symbols are themselves initiatory and attuning. There are additional initiations and attunements for the Angelic Symbols, but they are not necessary as they constitute more of an empowering factor. Such a form of an initiation can be asked directly by the individual from the angels and from his higher self, or he can receive it in a session by a teacher who has worked in depth with the Angelic Symbols. In both cases, the higher self and the angels are the ones to provide the initiations.

Can I come into contact with the angels via the Angelic Symbols?

Definitely. The symbols can bring the angels closer to us, or (to put it more correctly) they can bring us closer to them! They constitute an energetic language of light for angelic communication.

Can I combine the Angelic Symbols with Reiki or with other energy-healing methods?

Yes. Draw your favorite angelic symbol or the combination of the Angelic Symbols that you need while you are doing Reiki. Draw them energetically with your palm, or visualize or invoke them. They can be applied to you (Reiki self-healing) and others (Reiki sessions). They can also be applied from a distance (Reiki distant healing, second degree of Reiki) right after the use of the traditional symbols of Reiki. In a similar way, they can be used in all energy healing methods applied either to ourselves or others. They can be applied either in the beginning, during the session, at its completion, or at every stage, empowering and enhancing in this way all beneficial healing energies.

Can I combine them with invocations, prayers, or meditation?

Of course. Draw the Angelic Symbol you have chosen with your hand or visualize it before, during, or after your prayer or invocation. The same applies for meditation.

Can I draw the Angelic Symbols with colors and place them somewhere that is visible to other people? For instance, on the wall?

The answer is simple: Yes!

Some Angelic Symbols appeal to me more than others. Why is that?

That is because inside you, memories of angelic bliss, wholeness, and fulfillment are awakened. On an energy level, they are exactly what you need. Add them in your life as soon as possible!

Some Angelic Symbols seem strange to me or even repel me. Why is that?

You may not be directly connected with some symbols in the present state of your life. That is not a problem. Your preferences, needs, and aims may change in time. For instance, the symbols that you find unattractive now may appeal to you and be likable to you in the future. This is very probable as every day we become someone else, some-one different...a new, more complete, and more whole individual. We change, we are healed and transformed, we expand and we ascend, and we move forward and higher. We become celestialized, spiritualized, angelicalized, and divinized. We must always keep our minds and hearts open to the new.

Some Angelic Symbols seem indifferent to me, and I pass by them. Why?

Don't worry. They may seem interesting and prove useful to you in other cases.

When I draw the Angelic Symbols, I feel dizzy. Why is that happening?

This is because of their high vibration and energy. This shows you that they are actually starting to work. Be patient, keep going, insist, and enjoy the process. Release and let go of all tension and resistance; open up, relax, allow, and gently go with the flow.

When I draw the Angelic Symbols, I yawn intensely and I become teary. Why is that?

The symbols have cleansing and purifying effects. When you yawn or become teary, that means that you are cleansing yourself on an energy level and that you are releasing and throwing away what you no longer need and what blocks, limits, or burdens you.

When I draw the Angelic Symbols, I get a headache. Why?

The Angelic Symbols release mental tensions and blocks. This is a healing crisis, and it is for your own benefit. Just relax, and it will soon go away.

When I perform the Angelic Symbols, I feel intense heat, and I sweat or I feel cold. What does that mean?

When you feel hot sensations, it is the warm, vital energy of the Angelic Symbols that enfolds, permeates, and fills you, like the hot, life-giving sunlight. When you are cold, you may be unblocking yourself on an emotional level, or old beliefs and experiences may be "defrosting" and breaking so that they are sent away. It could also be the case that you perceive and receive higher frequencies of energy. If you feel intensely hot or fiery sensations, as if you are burning, the symbols work in a healing way directly on the physical level. It could also be the case that you are receiving some spiritual empowerment or initiation. Lie down and receive it as this is a highly beneficial gift and most often a supremely blissful, euphoric, and ecstatic experience.

When I use the Angelic Symbols, I feel chill or I shiver. What does that mean?

Your consciousness recognizes the exquisite angelic presences of pure light and unconditional love. Your spirit is awakened, and your soul rejoices.

How can I invoke the angels and the positive qualities in my life?

You can do this by consciously choosing to think positively; focusing on gratitude and the positive side of your existence; doing away with negative and limiting thoughts and

inferior-toxic emotions; sending away fear; and surrounding yourself with pure acceptance, love, peace, care, prayer, meditation, inner work, spiritual study, your clear and
focused intention, and the Angelic Symbols. You can do this by completely devoting
yourself to the good, healing, loving support and care of others and all beings.

How can I perceive angels or angelic energies near me?

A lot of people perceive angelic presences and energies either in their dreams or in
meditation, when they pray, or when they are in a state of deep relaxation. They also
perceive them when they are in a state of euphoria, higher inspiration, and expanded
consciousness. They perceive them outdoors in nature or in a state of emergency or
very often when they face a great danger.

The angels and their energies become noticeable in various ways, like when there is a
change in temperature, a cold sensation, a feeling of coolness, a sense of air, increas-
ing heat, or a sense of fire or burn. We may sense chill, numbness, waves in our body,
vibrations, spasms, pulses, or a sense of touch. We may feel pricks or pinches. We may
see in the space colors or light, bright spheres, a cloud, or a ray of light. We may hear
sounds, water, bells, melodies, or whispers. We may have some sort of intuitive message in our mind or some automatic knowledge, or we may hear a voice. We may see
a fleeting presence or suddenly sense euphoria, joy, peace, or liberation. We may feel
overemotional and weep. We may yawn or feel like laughing. We may get dizzy or lose
contact with the ground.

All of the above are signs that the angels and their bright, positive energies surround
us. It is important not to be scared but to invite them and welcome them with awe and
joy, with great love and gratitude. This will build our relationship with them, a most
valuable relationship that will bestow ultimate meaning, direction, and guidance to our
lives.

How do I know that the Angelic Symbols are positive or of positive origin? How do I know that they don't serve or are not connected with something negative, dark, or bad?

You can check them through your own wisdom, inner guidance, and discernment. Let
your intuition and inner voice guide you. Connect to your pure heart and ask that it

show this to you. Then you simply have to leave open all that is possible and trust so that you receive their amazing benefits. The symbols are of angelic origin indeed and have been received through spiritual direction and guidance in a time of intense inner work aimed at personal, collective, and planetary healing, as well as spiritual evolution. They are devoted to the higher good, and this is the only cause they serve. They are totally dedicated and completely attuned to the higher good through pure intention and strong focus, as well as through energy and spiritual means. The higher good of all is their cause and goal, their base and framework, their positive and bright essence. This can be personally proved to each individual through their direct experiential, personal use, the best and highest proof of them all.

Are the Angelic Symbols connected with magic?

Generally speaking, magic has been connected to negative issues and situations and in general terms has acquired in the collective subconscious a negative nuance, as magic has been used numerous times in the service of control and domination and the gratification of selfish ends and inferior passions. The Angelic Symbols aren't related to magic in this sense or context. On the other hand, if by the word "magic" we mean what is wondrous, metaphysical, and transcendental or some positive and bright healing path of love and service, then yes, the symbols are "magical"! They add more heavenly "magic" (beauty, awe, miracles) to Earth.

Is the work with the Angelic Symbols safe?

Yes, it is absolutely safe. There isn't any danger involved.

Can the Angelic Symbols offer healing?

The Angelic Symbols influence the etheric level, the aura, and the energy field of man, including the mental and the emotional levels. The physical body is gradually balanced, harmonized, and restored. As the aura and the energy field are fused with higher light and life-force energy, the mental and emotional levels are cleansed and illuminated, and the physical body reorganizes its powers, regaining its optimal function. Nevertheless, the symbols can't and shouldn't replace the field of conventional medicine and psychology or medical diagnosis and treatment. It is advisable that the symbols are used as complementary means along with conventional medicine. After all, medicine and psychology with all their amazing developments are also angelic gifts of the divine!

Do the symbols cause some form of cleansing and purification, either emotionally or physically?

Yes, all energetic and spiritual healing methods and practices do. As we begin to receive higher spiritual energies, it is possible to go through some form of physical cleansing or emotional purification, or both. They are only temporary, leading to an overall better and improved condition. The purification differs in intensity, kind, and level of manifestation and time duration from one individual to another and from one period of our lives to the other; it depends on what we carry inside and on how strongly we desire (on deeper levels) to advance and evolve. When we are in a state of cleansing, we should focus on and strengthen the virtues of patience, insistence, optimism, trust, and renewed positive vision and attitude.

What does the word "God" mean?

With complete spiritual freedom, the term "God" means what each individual perceives and understands in the way he understands and perceives it. The Angelic Symbols can be used by anyone, regardless of the manner he perceives the term and meaning of the word "God." We can say that God or the Divine is the Highest Principle of the Universe, the Ultimate Unity and Oneness that lies behind All, or the Supreme and Absolute Reality. It is inside, behind, and above all the phenomena and the whole of existence. It is the supreme, highest energy, essence, consciousness, and source of the world, of all and everything. Sacred religious texts, various spiritual and philosophical teachings, and personal experiences of esotericists, mystics, saints, and great masters teach us that "God is Love." Moreover, God is the highest level of reality: absolute (and not conditional), eternal (and not temporary), and infinite (and not finite). Its nature is supreme wisdom, supreme love, and supreme power. It is everywhere, and everything exists in this infinite reality. Inside it everything moves and breathes and has its being. The Divine or God is unknown and transcendental but at the same time personal and approachable inside ourselves and within our nature and essence, our soul, which is "in His own image and likeness." Man is on a cosmic journey toward the Divine, a journey of theosis, ascension, and unification of his being and consciousness with the Absolute Reality, Oneness, and Wholeness. A journey to Eden, toward the Primary Source. This is accomplished gradually, through a man's innumerable experiences in the material, physical world where he encounters conflicts and oppositions, good and evil, the positive and the negative, and pleasure and pain. It is accomplished through his alignment and recognition of the great spiritual-universal laws of life, such as the law of karma, the necessary relation between cause and effect (each cause/action produces an effect and each effect/condition has a cause). From a human perspective, nobody can say what or who God or the Divine is. But one can have a glimpse of its Supreme and Infinite Light, Life, and Love through deep meditative practices, ecstatic visions, and spiritual experiences that elevate and transform the human life, bestowing the highest and the greatest value, meaning, and purpose to it.

What if I don't agree with what has been stated above?

It's absolutely normal. All truths on Earth are relative because they are prisms and perspectives on Truth. The mind is a prism. Man is a prism. His experiences and knowledge are a prism. He never gets completely away from it. Nevertheless, this does not discourage us! All the (relatively relative) truths must be tested and experienced personally so that their validity and worth in human life are established. Man has to study the spiritual teachings and lessons in depth, compare, turn down, discover, synthesize, adopt, believe, doubt, transcend and, above all, experience them himself. Only in this way will the spiritual truth have a value and rightful position in his soul. In the journey of Life, man learns to inquire and investigate, doubt and challenge, and experience and believe (and not necessarily in this order!).

Do the angels replace God?

No. The angels are rays that lead to God, the Highest and Supreme Reality, the Highest and Supreme Consciousness. They lead to the Absolute Ecstatic Oneness and the Eternal Blissful Wholeness of All-That-Is. The angels are the manifestation of the absolute reality, highest source, principle, and power in various forms—God expressed and manifested. However, God or the Divine transcends the angels and everything infinitely, eternally, and supremely. It is an inconceivable—to the human mind—truth and reality.

Do I have to believe in God or the angels to use the Angelic Symbols?

No, but you can simply experiment and draw your own conclusions. However, you may be surprised by what you will experience or see opening in front of you. If angels or ideas, energies, and expressions of the Divine manifest in front of you, would you simply reject them to hold on to what is already known and apparently rational and reasonable? Or would you make a leap of faith and of consciousness? A leap inside your own self, the great unknown self, beyond all appearances and phenomena? A lot of people before you—all of them highly intelligent and courageous—have done it. It is absolutely safe, and you are absolutely safe. If you experience, take the leap!

Are the angels or the Angelic Symbols opposed to Christianity?

The angels constitute a part of the Christian religion and most other religions. Yet they aren't limited to them. After all, God and the angels don't have a religion and can appear and manifest to anyone! Who really knows God's Will? The Angelic Symbols are purely energy symbols of light, love, care, and healing, so they aren't contrary or incompatible with a spiritual or religious path.

Is there a possibility that I could invoke a dark or negative angel or that a dark or negative angel may appear as a bright and positive one?

No. This is about a work of a high level, high origin, and high-energy vibration. It has been given from high above for the purpose of healing and serving the highest good. Nothing negative can fit in this. Can a shadow appear itself as light? A shadow is a shadow, and light is light, so the difference is brighter than the sun! Nevertheless, if you do sense anything low or negative, then simply call Jesus Christ, Archangel Michael, or the Divine, God (the Highest Consciousness, Source, and Power) and ask to clean it or send it to the Light. That can happen while we ourselves are becoming purified from negative thought forms, beliefs, emotions, energies, and other influences. In that case, simply call the highest energies of light and ask for anything negative to be removed, released, and completely cleansed.

Is there a possibility that all this energetic or spiritual work is just autosuggestion, a placebo effect?

Once you start receiving energies and messages from the angels, once you start perceiving angelic presences and bright qualities, heaven, and earth will start playing a game:

they will start proving to you, in more than one way, that all of this is not just phenomena and impressions of your mind or brain. It is not the case of mere autosuggestion or placebo but a process and a plan of amazing truth, essence, beauty, and perfection that preexist and transcend you.

Is there a chance that I might lose my wits out of all this?

Man loses his wits due to the apparent cruelty of life, the material world, and everyday life, as well as due to pain, wounds, and afflictions from immense pressure and lack of freedom. Light, love, healing, spirituality, God and the angels, the higher dimensions and the higher states of consciousness, prayer, meditation, and engagement with the esoteric, and metaphysics not only confirm our wits, giving them luminous purity and clarity of mind, but also offer inconceivable beauty, tranquility, freedom, and balance to ourselves and our lives. A life without a quest is a life with no meaning and value. After all, the human being is the one looking within and also above and beyond. It is the nature of the consciousness itself to question, wonder, admire, and wish knowledge and truth inside, behind, above, and beyond all worldly appearances and phenomena.

When, how, and why were the Angelic Symbols given?

The writer had been working on a daily basis for many years in intensive ways with the spiritual energies and new ways of healing and personal development. Between 2008 and 2010, after his request and after specific inspiration and spiritual guidance he received an ensemble of symbols, prayers, invocations, meditations, techniques, and initiations. He recorded them in a series of books under the heading "Celestial Gifts." This material was bestowed on him so that his energy, life, and spirituality would become enlightened, enhanced, and enriched, as would the energy, life, and spirituality of the people close to him and of all those who wish to come into contact with all these gifts! His sole wish and intention is the healing of the planet and of all people. This work as a whole, along with the thoughts, emotions, inspirations, actions, and choices, focus on that wish and intention.

What do the Angelic Symbols mean? For instance, what does "Angelic Love" or "Angelic Light" or "Angelic Abundance" mean, and what happens when I look at them, visualize them, or draw them?

While we view or picture in our mind or draw with our hand the symbol "Angelic Love," we attune ourselves with love in its angelic vibration and in its angelic form in the way the angels experience it and transmit it. We awaken the angelic qualities and vibrations of love and its higher and pure self beyond all phenomena, opposition, and our own limitations.

By drawing the symbol, we bring this energy to our hands, our aura, and our being. We express it and manifest it inside us and around us. It is a healing process. A small enlightenment! We receive angelic blessings. We experience spiritual empowerment. The same goes for all the symbols. By gazing at the ensemble of symbols, studying them, going through each symbol separately, and drawing it with the hand, or visualizing it in our mind, we feel and experience the corresponding energies: the pure, bright, and beneficial-for-human-existence energies. The Angelic Symbols are symbols that ground, manifest, and transmit the higher aspects of every meaning, condition, and property to which they refer.

For instance, by drawing the symbol of "Angelic Maths," we attune ourselves to the higher or divine aspect of maths—the energy of their beauty and their truth. By drawing the symbols of the "Angelic Healing of the Chakras," we charge and enlighten our energy centers with higher qualities and vibrations. In a similar way, by drawing the "Angelic Ascension," we elevate our being toward the light. By drawing "Angelic Protection," we bring protection to us, and by drawing "Angelic Abundance," we attract and realize abundance in our lives.

By drawing the Angelic Symbols, we allow the angels to enter more lively and directly than ever in our lives! We speak their energy language, which is a spiritual and geometrical language beyond all words, and we welcome them. At the same time, we express our angelic (pure, higher, real, essential) being. We make our lives angelic; we become angels on Earth.

Do I have to know what the Angelic Symbols mean? Some symbols are incomprehensible to me. For instance, what do the terms "Angelic Body," "Angelic Speech," "Angelic Structures," "Angelic Particles," "Angelic Time," and "Angelic Pyramid" mean?

There are no specific explanations. As you view or visualize or draw every symbol, try to feel and experience its quality, vibration, energy, flow, effect, and state it creates. Observe. Become attentive and sensitive and observe the feelings, thoughts, sensations, and insights. Observe carefully everything that happens inside and around you. Be attentive and aware. Contemplate and meditate. Ask yourself, "What does 'Angelic Body' mean?" How do you understand it? What could it possibly mean? Put your higher mind, intelligence, and intuition in action and motion! What does each symbol mean to you? What could it mean, and where could it help? What kind of energy does it have when you use it? How can the symbols be combined, and for what purpose each time? Act intuitively. Let the angels and the symbols guide you. There is no mistake. All is energy. All is light. All is love. In complete freedom and with no trace of fear, ask yourself. Explore and experiment, imagine, guess, grasp, and experience. You'll find all the answers and everything you are looking for.

I have read that the archangels Azrael and Samael are angels of death and subsequently negative/dark angels. Is it proper to invoke them or use their symbols?

The symbols, meditations, and the angelic invocations connect us with the cosmic powers the angels represent, express, and manifest. Archangels Azrael and Samael manifest human fear and its cleansing, release, and transcendence. They manifest lower or negative feelings and thoughts and their transmutation, healing, and overcoming. They are related and represent the material level, life in the material world, and death as its completion. Death is not something dark and negative; it is a transition, crossing over to something new. It is a part of life. It is life's natural consequence for new and more life to emerge. Life and death are aspects of the material dimension and the higher dimensions. In Spirit there is life and only life. It is boundless, never-ending, eternal life.

By drawing the symbols of Azrael and Samael or by invoking them, usually in combination with the higher archangels like Michael (the Divine Will, Divine Power), we cleanse the inferior aspects of our own self and the way we perceive matter, fear, the unknown, death, darkness, evil, and negativity; the negative pole exists, and we must come face to face with it, understand it, deal with it, and, finally, heal and transcend it. The symbols and the invocations cannot provoke anything negative. As spiritual technology of light, they purify it and transmute it. These archangels are part of the Divine Plan, and cooperation with them is not only unavoidable but necessary and essential for all mystics, healers, and great teachers and for those who wish more than anything to be of service to their fellow beings and who want the happiness and enlightenment of all, in addition to supreme unification with the Divine.

A sacred secret of esotericism and mysticism is this: these two archangels, Azreal and Samael, are angels of matter. They can provoke, in alignment with the higher powers of spirit, light, love (the higher archangels, such as Michael, Gabriel, and Raphael) the miraculous healing of heavy, dense matter: of the physical body itself. This is possible because they are the ones providing the physical body with dense matter as the angelic masters of materialization.

Who are the transcendental unknown angels (Groups A, B, and C) mentioned in the corresponding Angelic Symbols?

We don't know. They are transcendental beings of infinite light and the human consciousness can reach only to the coasts of their oceanic energy. They aren't known to humanity empirically. Their symbols have been given as a first approach and acquaintance. These symbols can derive some of their infinite divine light.

Who are the angels of the twelve rays? What are the twelve rays?

They are twelve main streams of divine energy of the great spectrum of light. Information about them can be found in esoteric philosophy. Few are the things that man can comprehend and experience in relation to them. Their angels are their representatives and masters of these streams. A brief and very simple presentation of the twelve rays and their angels according to esotericism is given below. A disciple is invited and encouraged to meditate on their meanings and essences.

The following list consists of each of the twelve rays, its corresponding color (which can be used to visualize and connect with it), its name and theme (its major virtue, energy, focus), and its representative angels.

First Ray (red): Will and Power. Archangel Michael and Lady Faith

Second Ray (blue): Love and Wisdom. Archangel Jophiel and Lady Constance

Third Ray (yellow): Active intelligence and Intellect. Archangel Chamuel and Lady Charity

Fourth Ray (green): Harmony, Beauty, Art, and Will. Archangel Gabriel and Lady Hope

Fifth Ray (orange): Concrete Knowledge and Science. Archangel Raphael and Mother Mary

Sixth Ray (indigo): Devotion, Idealism, and Inner Wisdom. Archangel Uriel and Lady Grace

Seventh Ray (violet): Transmutation, Alchemy, and Ceremonial Order. Archangel Zadkiel and Lady Amethyst

Eighth Ray (aquamarine, sea green): Catharsis and Purification. Archangels of Psychic Clearing/Purification, Haniel

Ninth Ray (turquoise): Light-Body Attraction/Activation. Archangels of emotional intelligence and creativity, Tzaphkiel

Tenth Ray (pearl white, golden): Light-Body Grounding, Connection to the Soul and Monad. Archangels of the Holy Spirit, Sandalphon

Eleventh Ray (bright pink-orange, golden touches): Bridge to the New Age. Archangel Metatron

Twelfth Ray (golden): Grounding of the New Age and the Christ Consciousness. Archangels of Christ, Jeremiel

Who are the Angels of Christ and the Angels of the Holy Mother?

They are pure, holy, and sacred angels that are related to Christ and the Holy Mother, with their earthly life or with their inner eternal energy and essence. They could be related to the earthly life of Jesus and Virgin Mary or the cosmic energy of Christ (Christ consciousness) and the Holy Mother (feminine aspect of existence, of divinity). Individuals who feel close to Jesus and the Virgin Mother are similarly close to these angels. Moreover, they could be or could be identified with the known angels of the Bible.

Who are the multidimensional angels and the angels of dimensions (fifth, sixth...eleventh, twelfth dimensions)?

The multidimensional angels could be angels who exist simultaneously in numerous dimensions or have the ability to travel to numerous ones. They could also be angels who build and maintain the dimensions, distinguishing and protecting them or aligning and uniting them. The angels of each dimension are responsible correspondingly for each one. Moreover, they are the angels who we as human beings perceive in each different dimension.

Who are the angels from Pleiades and from Sirius?

They are angels who are connected with these constellations. If your soul has travelled to them or plans to do so, then you will probably be feeling an attraction to these constellations. These angels could possibly be or be identified with the known archangels and angelic orders, maybe in a different manifestation of theirs—depending on the needs and the perception of the residents of these stars!

Who are the Angels of Shamballa?

They are virtually all the known archangels. They work—probably in their most human or humanlike manifestations—with the Ascended Masters (saints who have been ascended and great masters and teachers of humanity) to promote the healing and the growth of consciousness on Earth. Shamballa is the higher self of humanity, the sacred spiritual center of the great teachers' wisdom, power, and love. As a spiritual place, it exists in a higher dimension of reality: the sixth dimension, the transcendental dimension of pure light and Spirit.

Can I connect and communicate with my guardian angel through the corresponding symbol? If so, how should I use it?

Yes. Sit comfortably and take some deep breaths, relaxing more and more. Draw with your right palm the symbol of the guardian angel in the air in front of you and then ask him mentally to come close to you. Relax more and become open and receptive. Open your heart like a flower that is blooming, and feel love and gratitude. Visualize yourself being surrounded only by pure light. Intend that light (and only light) surrounds and fills you. Feel this taking place. Think about your guardian angel, and connect with him on an energy level, again through your intention. Repeat the symbol by drawing it once more energetically with your palm in the air. You can do it a third time if you believe it is necessary, or visualize it in bright gold or white light. Stay as long as you like in this pure, radiant, bright energy. Ask to feel your guardian angel or see him; ask for spiritual protection and guidance; ask to receive answers to your questions or healing and direction in your life. At the end, send him your greatest and highest love, and give thanks! Do this practice daily—at least seven days in a row, without any hurry or pressure, in an atmosphere of joy and awe—to cultivate a more intense energy connection and a deeper spiritual experience.

Can I use the symbol of Archangel Michael for protection? How?

Yes. Draw with your hand in the air the symbol of Archangel Michael, and ask him mentally to come and protect you or your space. Repeat the symbol many times, as many as you intuitively feel are necessary. Stay long enough in this energy. Thank Archangel Michael truly and warmheartedly. Affirm powerfully that Archangel Michael is 100 percent with you and that he offers total and complete protection on all levels—to you and your space.

Can I use the symbol of Archangel Raphael for healing?

Yes, in the same way: Draw with your hand in the air the symbol of Archangel Raphael and mentally ask him to come and heal you or another person. Repeat the symbol many times more, as many as you intuitively feel are necessary. Visualize yourself being surrounded only by light—pure, vital, bright light. It is the light of life and etheric vitality. Do it meditatively. See and feel it as clearly as possible or simply intend it. Relax deeply and stay as much as you can in this bright energy of pure life. Lovingly thank Archangel Raphael from deep within your heart and soul, and powerfully affirm that he's 100 percent with you and offering to you (or to another person) total and complete healing on all levels.

Some symbols are called "Angelic Healing of the Chakras" (of the first, second, third chakras, etc.). What are the chakras?

There are seven major chakras. They constitute the main energy centers in the etheric or energy body of man that permeates the physical body and provides it with life-force energy, power, and vitality. The etheric body includes the meridians (energy channels) and the aura (outer layer or shield). *Chakra* in Sanskrit means "wheel" because the energy centers resemble discs or vortexes that swirl, channel, and transfer vital energy to the corresponding places in the physical body. The chakras are found on the central channel of the body (central pillar of light), the *sushumna*, and is parallel to the spinal cord.

The following list is a basic presentation of the seven major chakras: their location on the etheric/physical body, their color, and their main themes and functions.

First chakra

Color: red
Location: base of the spinal cord, coccyx, and perineum
Physical correspondence: genetic code, bones, and legs
Main themes: connection to the earth, material life, grounding, family, DNA, ancestors, physical strength, basic needs, survival, abundance, and protection

Second chakra

Color: orange
Location: pelvic area, one palm below the navel
Physical correspondence: lower abdomen, reproductive organs
Main themes: sexual energy, work, creativity, joy, relationships, vitality, energy of life

Third chakra

Color: yellow
Location: solar plexus and stomach
Physical correspondence: stomach, upper abdomen, and digestion
Main themes: will, power, self-esteem, self-confidence, acceptance, balance, ego, and personality

Fourth chakra

Color: green
Location: middle of the chest
Physical correspondence: chest, lungs, heart, immune, and the circulatory and respiratory systems
Main themes: emotions, harmony, peace, freedom, and love

Fifth chakra

Color: blue
Location: base of the neck
Physical correspondence: neck
Main themes: Expression, communication, truth, and peace

Sixth chakra

Color: deep blue, indigo, and purple
Location: middle of the forehead

Physical correspondence: brain, head, and face
Main themes: thought, imagination, intuition, insight, and perception

Seventh chakra

Color: white and violet
Location: top of the head
Physical correspondence: nervous system
Main themes: consciousness, awareness, and spirituality; connection to the universe, nature, and the higher power; transcendence; and oneness.

Apart from these main seven energy centers, numerous secondary ones also exist. There are minor chakras in the palms, the elbows, the cheeks, the shoulders, the back, the knees, the feet, the left and right side of the chest, the abdomen, and the pelvis—on the left and right side of all seven major energy centers.

Two additional important energy centers are the **soul chakra** or **soul star** and the Earth chakra or Earth star:

Soul chakra

Color: golden
Location: a meter above the head
Main themes: qualities of the soul, higher self, potential, possibilities, and divine plan

Earth chakra

Color: silver
Location: a meter below the feet
Main themes: physical incarnation, actualization, manifestation, fulfillment of the soul's plan and life's purpose, greater connection to Earth, and the power to adapt.

The Angelic Symbols can stimulate and awaken, cleanse and purify, activate and charge, illuminate and enlighten, and empower and balance all chakras, offering more life-force energy and vitality to the etheric and physical body and subsequently to all levels of one's being. They can enhance overall well-being, health, and happiness.

How can I perform a complete energy healing session with the Angelic Symbols?

There are some simple steps in order to perform a complete energy healing process using the Angelic Symbols.

First Method of Angelic Symbols Energy Healing

Prepare your space, both on a physical and energy level. Let some fresh air and sunlight in; clean it; and make sure that it is pleasant, tidy, and harmonious. Light white candles, scent your home naturally with pure essential oils, and put on relaxing music. You can energetically draw your favorite symbols in the air and the walls.

Prepare yourself, as well, on a physical and energy level: Have a shower or a bath (use thick salt, which purifies the energy) and make sure that you are extra clean! At the same time, picture in your mind a bright white light washing you all away, internally and externally.

Be in a state of pure love, respect, and gratitude for the person receiving the session.

Ask from the individual who will receive the session to lie down comfortably. That individual should be dressed.

Ask from him/her to take some full breaths, deeply and slowly, close his or her eyes, and relax.

Place your hands in prayer position, joined in front of your chest.

In your mind, call the angels of God who are related to healing. Become receptive, open yourself, and express love and gratitude to the great angels of the Divine. Invite and welcome them in the greatest love, awe, and joy.

Draw energetically the following Angelic Symbols in front of you or above the person (over his seventh chakra or over his entire body): *Guardian Angel, Archangel Michael, Archangel Gabriel, Archangel Raphael, Archangel Uriel, Archangel Zadkiel,* and *Healing Angels.*

Pray or ask for the highest good. Pray the best for the individual.

Visualize pure, bright white light surrounding and embracing the person. It is the light of life.

Visualize the warm, vital light permeating the person and filling him or her.

Very gently place your hands on the top of his or her head.

Visualize the symbol of *Angelic Energy* in white or gold light. Gently keep your hands there for a few minutes and relax, observing whatever is happening and everything you feel.

Then, gently place your hands on other parts. Place them on the eyes, the ears, the back of the head, the neck, the chest, the abdomen, the pelvis, the palms, the knees, and the feet of the person.

Be gentle, and apply no pressure at all. Place hands wherever else it is necessary or wherever you feel the need to, but never on the genitals or breasts.

The same hand positions (with possible variations) are also widely used in Reiki and other methods of energy healing.

Leave your hands in each position for three to five minutes. Be gentle, and never press. Relax and be attentive, open, and sensitive. Use your intuition. Notice the sensations in your palms and your thoughts and emotions. Be hyperaware of everything internally and externally. Proceed meditatively.

In every position, visualize the symbol of *Angelic Energy* in white or gold light.

If you wish, you can draw it with your hand on every position. Do it from a short distance from the person's body on his or her aura.

Furthermore, in these different positions, you can visualize or draw the symbol of *Angelic Love* or the symbol of *Angelic Light*. All three symbols, *Angelic Energy, Angelic Love,* and *Angelic Light,* work perfectly for energy healing.

Finally, place again your hands in prayer position and visualize the light surrounding and permeating the person once more. Visualize him or her being completely healthy, strong, relaxed, and happy, having received all that he or she needs.

Think the greatest positive thoughts and feel the highest positive emotions you can about the person.

Thank all the angels lovingly and wholeheartedly.

Take a deep breath, and feel completely renewed, revitalized, and rejuvenated.

Give time to the person to wake up and fully return.

Offer him or her glass of water, and have one yourself. Wash your hands and face.

This session can be repeated several days in a row or consistently, such as twice a week.

Other directions
1. During the session, you can intuitively use additional symbols.
2. Instead of lying down, the person receiving the session can sit on a chair. Adjust the hand positions accordingly.
3. All the hand positions can be performed from a short distance as well, without touching the person directly but while keeping the palms on the receiver's aura. This can be performed if you aren't familiar with the person or if you or the other person does not desire any physical contact. Just hold your palms in a short distance from the body, a few centimeters above it. This auric method is equally as powerful as the touch method.

Second Method of Angelic Symbols Energy Healing

Perform the same physical and energetic preparation for yourself and your space.

Draw the symbols for the *Angelic Healing of the Chakras*, one on each chakra.

Draw them in short distance from the person's body.

There are nine symbols: seven for the main seven chakras, one for the soul chakra, and one for the Earth chakra.

Use them all, one after the other: Starting by the seventh chakra on the top of the head, proceed to the sixth on the forehead, the fifth on the neck, the fourth on the chest, the third on the stomach, the second on the pelvic area, and the first at the base of the torso. Then draw the soul chakra, about a meter above the head, and the earth chakra, about a meter below the feet.

Next, draw the following symbols over the entire body: *Deep Healing, Karma Healing, Aura Healing, Emotional Healing, Mental Healing, Spiritual Healing,* and *Cellular Healing.*

You may draw additional symbols if you feel guided to.

Draw all the symbols with your hands on the person's aura or on positions with possible blockages or where you judge it is vital, following your intuition. Additionally, draw them on the body parts that the person has informed you that he wishes to be cleared, healed, empowered, or balanced.

If you wish, you may visualize the symbols in white or golden light instead of drawing them with your palm.

Keep every symbol long enough on the person's aura, holding your palm there or by holding the symbol mentally in visualization so that the symbol can act and channel its beneficial energies.

In the end, complete the session in the same way you did in the first method described above.

Third Method of Angelic Symbols Energy Healing

Ask the receiver to choose twelve symbols by taking time to skim through the book.

Draw them on a piece of paper, and after preparing yourself accordingly, visualize them or draw them energetically with your palm on the person's aura or on specific spots. Repeat the symbols you intuitively feel the person needs most.

Conclude the session as before.

Fourth Method of Angelic Symbols Energy Healing

Choose twelve or more symbols for the person. Draw them on him or her. When it comes to which ones to choose, follow your intuition and angelic guidance.

Note: The four methods of Angelic Symbols energy healing can be combined, adapted, or enhanced.

Important notes for all energy sessions
1. Never promise any kind of cure other than holistic relaxation and energy clearing, empowerment, and balance. Never interfere with medical or psychological diagnosis and treatment. Energy work does not in any way substitute for medical or psychological diagnosis and treatment.
2. Do not consume alcohol or any kind of recreational drugs for at least twenty-four hours prior to any energy work.

You can perform any of the above methods on yourself by self-applying all the steps.

Is there a more advanced or special method to perform an energy healing session with the Angelic Symbols?

Yes, there are many. You can discover or create them through inspiration from the symbols themselves. Combinations of similar or related symbols and combinations of different symbols give rise to new techniques and methods aimed at a deeper energy work and manifestation. As you will be practicing on a daily basis and in a more dedicated manner with the symbols, you will receive relevant and specific healing guidance for yourself and for the people you work with energetically and spiritually.

Some symbols are related to specific archangels (Michael, Gabriel, Raphael, etc.) and angelic orders (seraphim, cherubim, thrones, etc.). How can I learn more about them?

Please consult the appendix at the end of this book. It offers a detailed account of all major and the most well-known archangels and angelic orders.

How can I expand this work and advance?

Study the other two volumes of this angelic book series: Celestial Gifts: *Angelic Invocations* and *Angelic Meditations & Mysticism*.

Is there any further advice?

I. Love yourself. Love yourself sincerely, truly, deeply, wholly, infinitely, totally, supremely, and absolutely. Love others as you love yourself. And love the world, life, existence, Spirit, God, the Divine, and All That Is with the same love.

II. Show, express, and actively manifest all of this energy of love by daily performing good deeds of true loving-kindness in service to all.

Angelic Symbols

Angelic Love

Angelic Light

Angelic Guidance

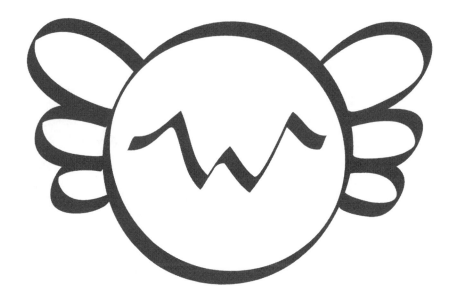

Angelic Abundance

Angelic Serenity

Angelic Protection

Angelic Joy

Angelic Healing

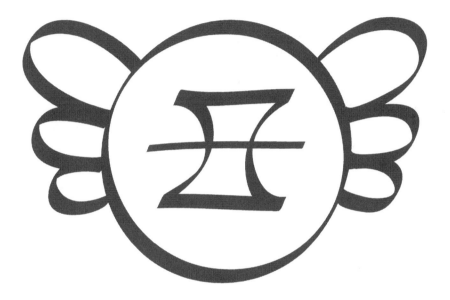

Angelic Peace

Angelic Justice

Angelic Mercy

Angelic Dominion

Angelic Relaxation

Angelic Energy

Angelic Dream

Angelic Sleep

Angelic Prediction

Angelic Grace

Angelic Freedom

Angelic Truth

Angelic Expression-Communication

Angelic Perfection

Angelic Principles

Angelic Laws

Angelic Scripts

Angelic Flow

Angelic Structures

Angelic Mathematics

Angelic Insight

Angelic Intuition

Angelic Detoxification

Angelic Body

Angelic Health

Angelic Miracle

Angelic Speech

Angelic Art

Angelic Knowledge

Angelic Awakening

Angelic Particles

Angelic Matter

Angelic Colors

Angelic Sound

Angelic Rays

Angelic Spheres

Angelic Pyramid

Angelic Music

Angelic Dance

Angelic Flying

Angelic Elevation

Angelic Beauty

Angelic Life

Angelic Happiness

Angelic Good Fortune

Angelic Wealth

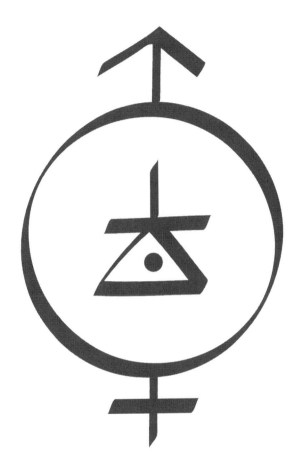

Angelic Friendship

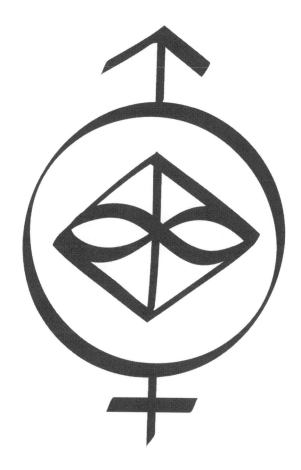

Angelic Romance

Angelic Work

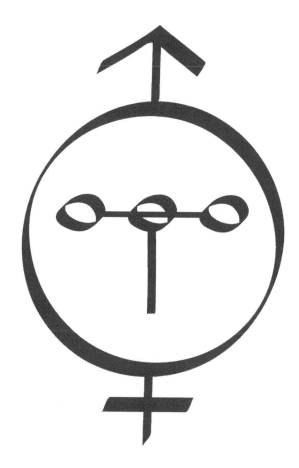

Angelic Purpose

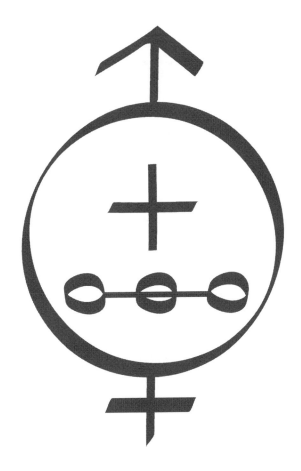

Angelic Adaptation

Angelic House

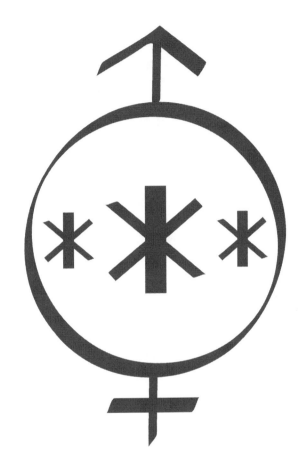

Angelic Spiritual Powers

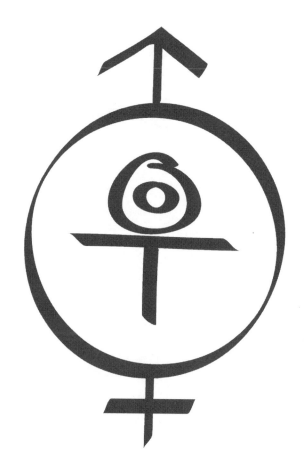

Angelic Talents

Angelic Consciousness

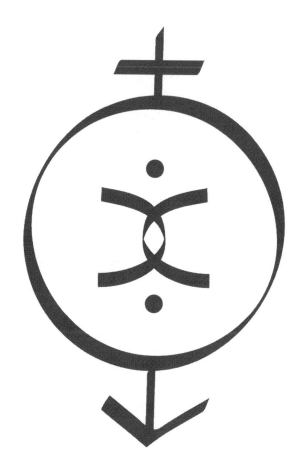

Angelic Unity

Angelic Ecstasy

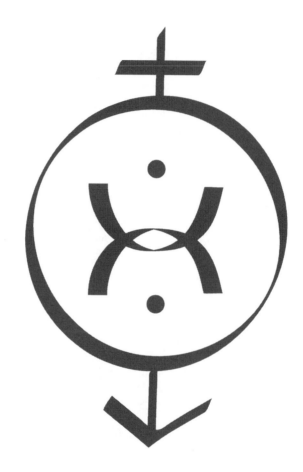

Angelic Forgiveness

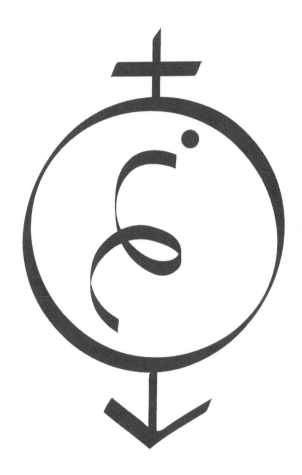

Angelic Repentance

Angelic Expansion

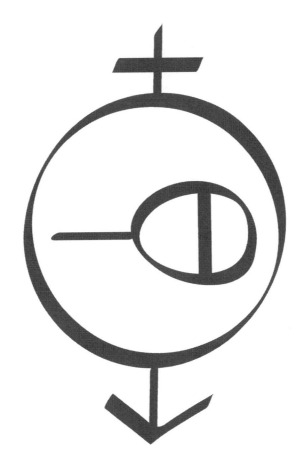

Angelic Completion

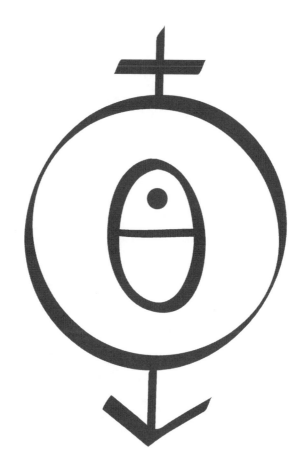

Angelic Blessing

Angelic Wisdom

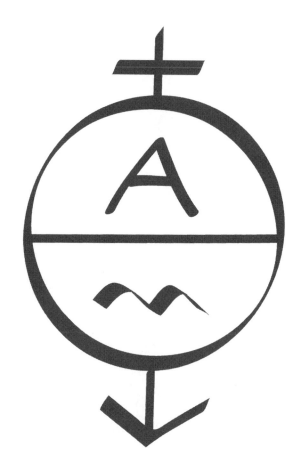

Angelic Power

Angelic Past

Angelic Future

Angelic Present

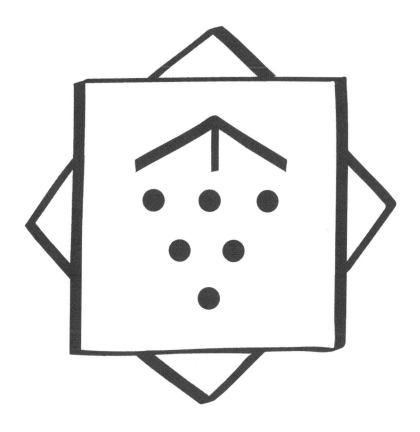

Angelic Time

Angelic Play and Playfulness

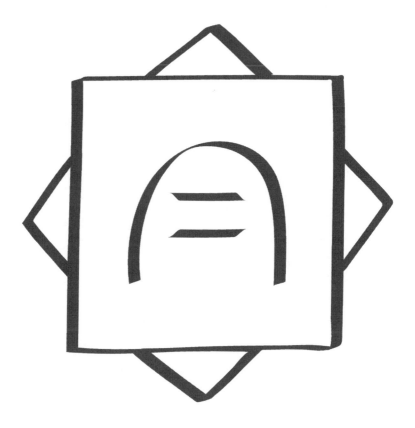

Angelic Resting and Rejuvenation

Angelic Satisfaction

Angelic Fullness

Angelic Courage

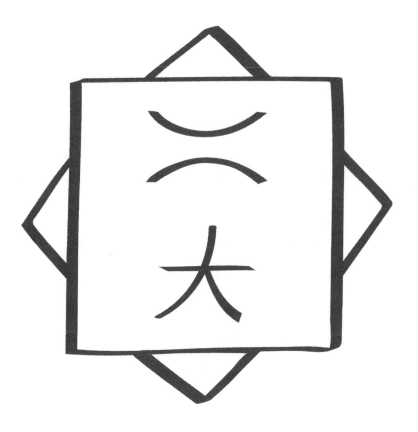

Angelic Hope

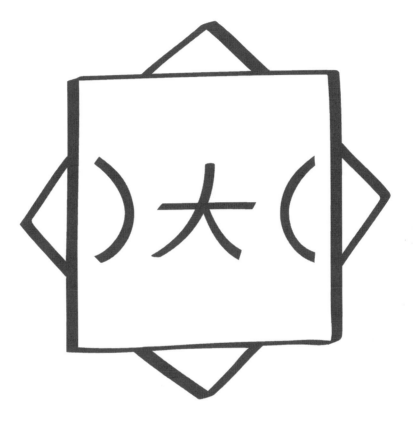

Angelic Brotherhood and Sisterhood

Angelic Deep Healing

Angelic Kindness

Angelic Compassion

Angelic Togetherness

Angelic Aura

Angelic Aura Healing

Angelic Emotional Healing

Angelic Mental Healing

Angelic Spiritual Healing

Angelic Cellular Healing

Angelic DNA

Angelic Healing
of the 1st Chakra

Angelic Healing
of the 2nd Chakra

Angelic Healing
of the 3rd Chakra

Angelic Healing
of the 4th Chakra

Angelic Healing
of the 5th Chakra

Angelic Healing
of the 6th Chakra

Angelic Healing
of the 7th Chakra

Angelic Healing
of the Soul Chakra

Angelic Healing
of the Earth Chakra

Angelic Relationship Healing

Angelic Healing of
Life, Direction, Purpose

Angelic Karma Healing

Angelic Clearing of Negative Influence

Angelic Purification of Negative Energy

Angelic Easiness

Angelic Transcendence

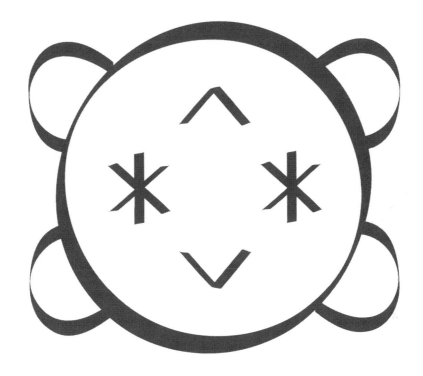

Angelic Inspiration

Angelic Answers

Angelic Message

Angelic Manners

Angelic Rehabilitation

Angelic Order and Organization

Angelic Study and Learning

Angelic Providence

Angelic Help

Angelic Realm, Level, Dimension

Angelic Heavenly Stairway / Bridge

Angelic Thought

Angelic Emotion

Angelic Spirit

Angelic Soul

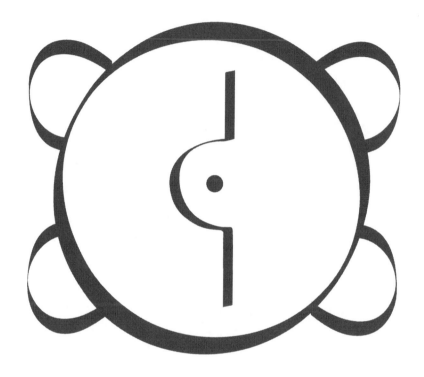

Angelic Creativity

Angelic Child

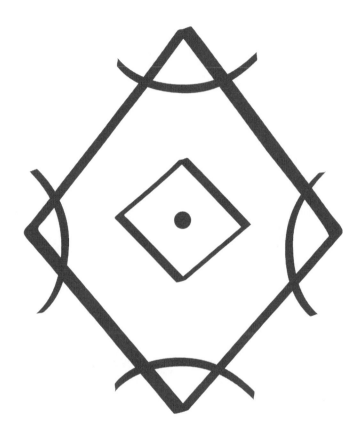

Angelic Centre

Angelic Enlightenment

Angelic Ascension

Angelic Release

Angelic Cleansing

Angelic Purity

Angelic Relationships

Angelic Character

Angelic Intention

Angelic Focus

Angelic Priority

Angelic Earth

Angelic Water

Angelic Fire

Angelic Air

Angelic Baptism

Angelic Painkiller

Angelic Planetary Enlightenment

Angelic Planetary Healing

Angelic Repairing

Angelic Recreation and Reconstruction

Angelic Invention

Angelic Memory

Angelic Endurance

Angelic Courage

Angelic Optimism

Angelic Empowerment

Angelic Initiation

Angelic Attunement

Angelic Harmonization

Angelic Harmony

Angelic Balance

Angelic Healing Powers

Angelic Self-Healing

Angelic Family

Angelic Connection

Angelic Meditation

Angelic Faith

Angelic Trust

Angelic Honesty

Angelic Warmth

Angelic Gratitude

Angelic Secrets

Angelic Sacredness

Angelic Holiness

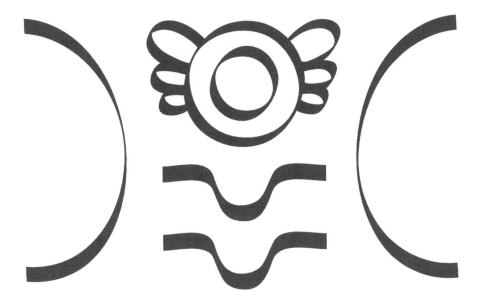

Angelic Openness

Angelic Acceptance

Angelic Activation

Angelic Lessons

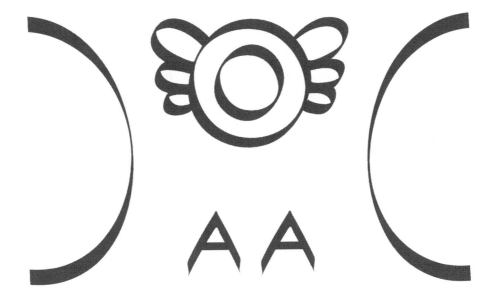

Angelic Codes

Angelic Grounding

Angelic Manifestation
and Materialization

Seraphim

Cherubim

Thrones (Ophanim)

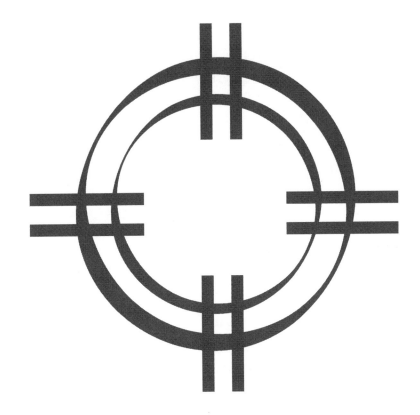

Dominions

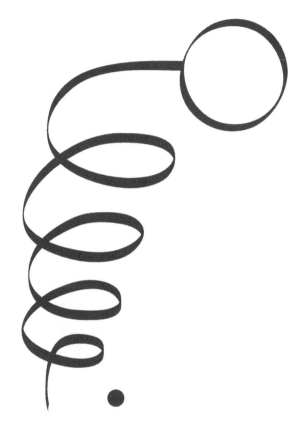

Virtues

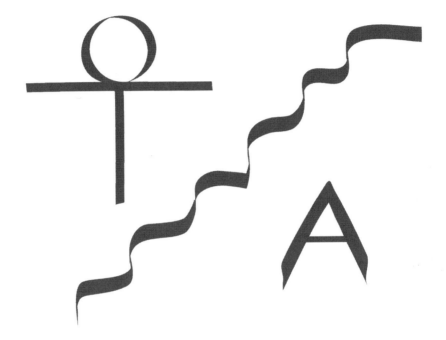

Powers (Authorities)

Principalities (Rulers)

Archangels

Angels

Archangel Michael

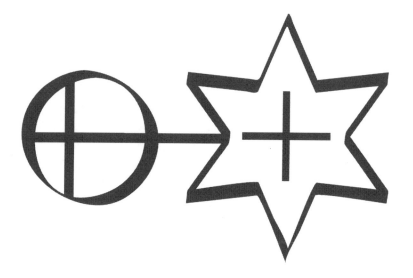

Archangel Gabriel

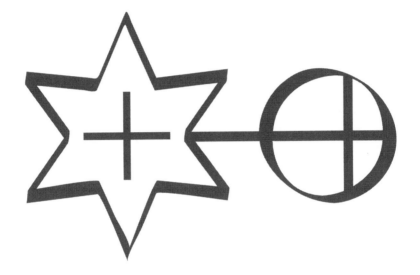

Archangel Raphael

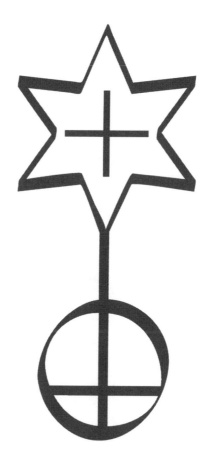

Archangel Uriel

Archangel Sandalphon

Archangel Metatron

Archangel Haniel

Archangel Chamuel (Camael)

Archangel Raziel

Archangel Ariel

Archangel Tzaphkiel

Archangel Zadkiel

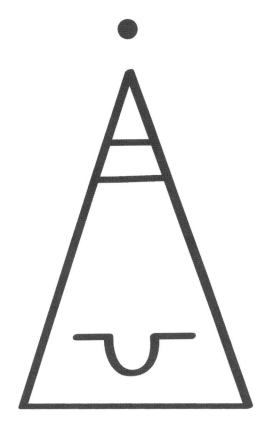

Archangel Jophiel

Archangel Jeremiel

Archangel Samael

Archangel Azrael

Archangel Raguel

Guardian Angel

Shekhinah

Elohim

Nature Angels

Earth Angels

Water Angels

Fire Angels

Air Angels

Healing Angels

Protection Angels

Guidance Angels

Karma Angels

Life Purpose Angels

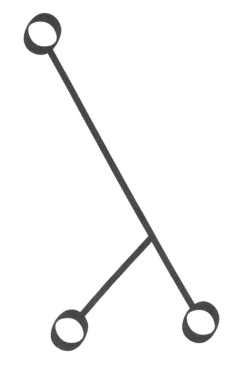

Abundance Angels

Romance Angels

Family Angels

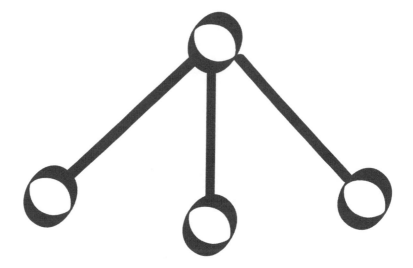

Animal Angels

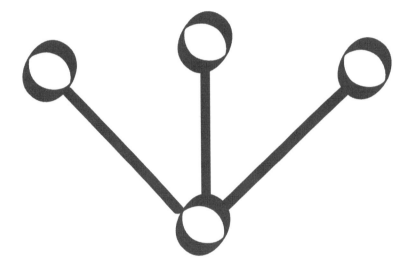

Crystals Angels

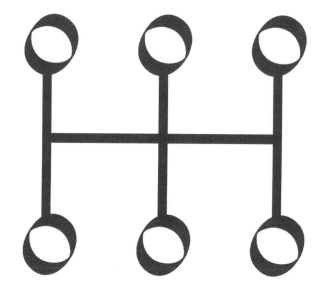

Plants Angels

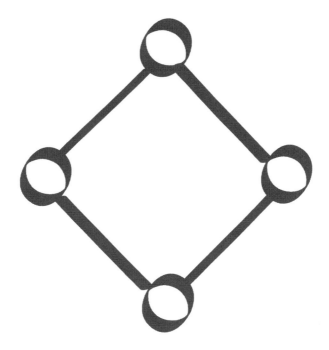

Sun Angels

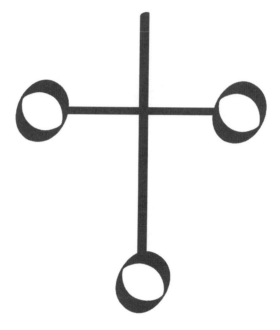

Moon Angels

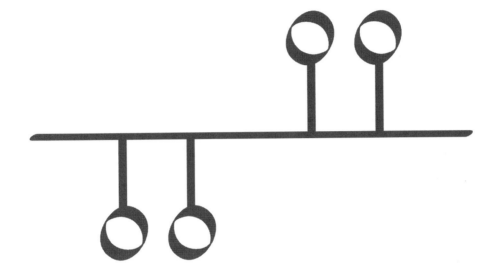

Knowledge & Wisdom Angels

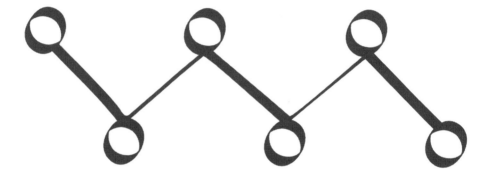

Enlightenment & Ascension Angels

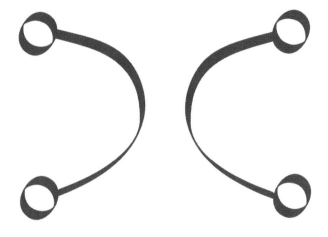

Music Angels

Arts Angels

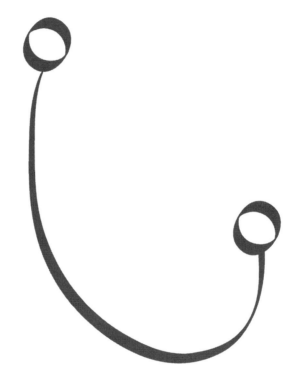

Sciences Angels

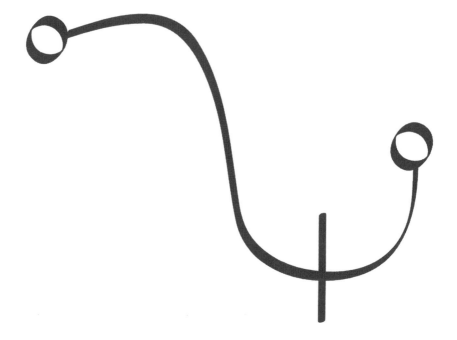

Transmutation Angels

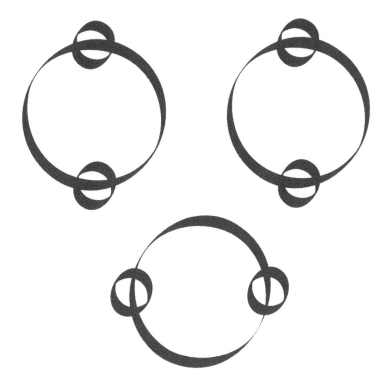

Colors Angels

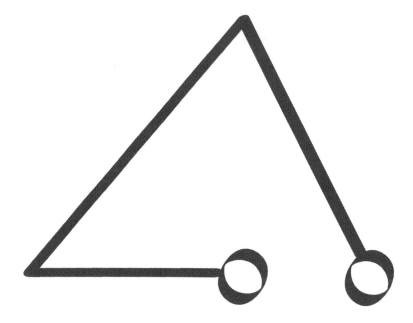

Symbols Angels

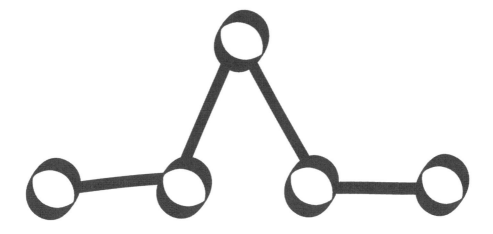

Stars Angels

Insight Angels

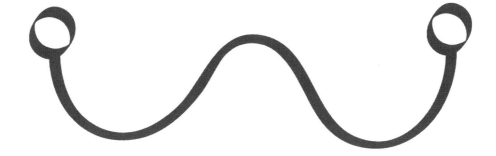

Laughter & Play Angels

Happiness Angels

Holy Spirit Angels

Christ Angels

Logos Angels

Holy Mother,
Divine Mother Angels

Yin/Yang Angels

White Light Angels

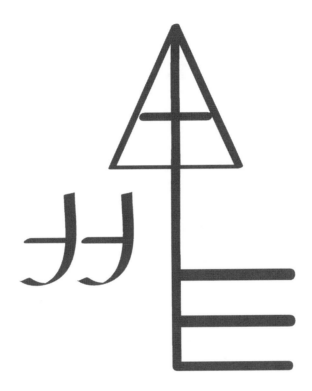

Golden Light Angels

Violet Light / Flame Angels

First Ray Angels

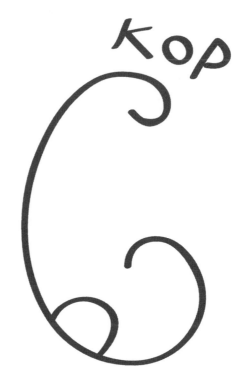

Second Ray Angels

Third Ray Angels

Fourth Ray Angels

Fifth Ray Angels

Sixth Ray Angels

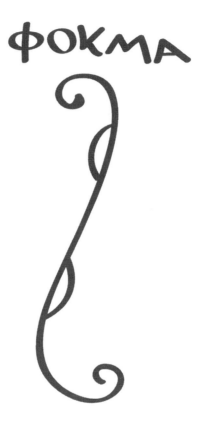

ΦΟΚΜΑ

Seventh Ray Angels

ANTIEM

Eighth Ray Angels

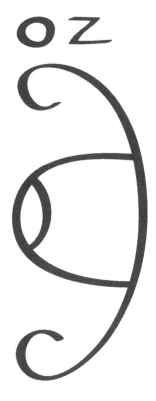

Ninth Ray Angels

Ro

Tenth Ray Angels

Eleventh Ray Angels

RUIPIZ

Twelfth Ray Angels

Unknown Transcendental Angels, Group A

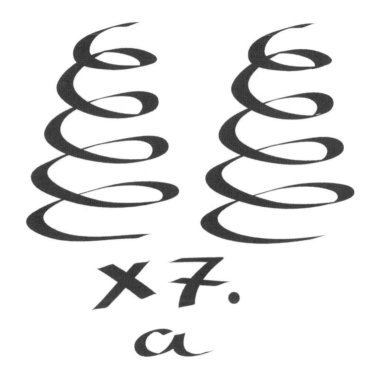

Transcendental Superlight Angels

Unknown Angels of the Source, Group B

Nirvana Angels,
Group C

Ninth Dimension Angels,
Eloha Angels

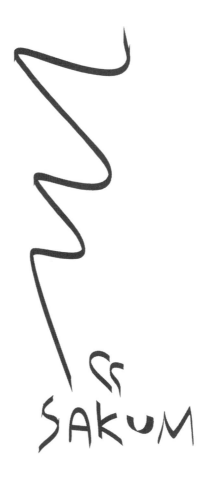

Eighth Dimension Angels

Multidimensional Angels

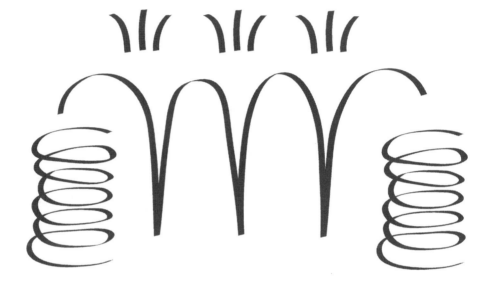

Seventh Dimension Angels

Fifth Dimension Angels

Sixth Dimension Angels

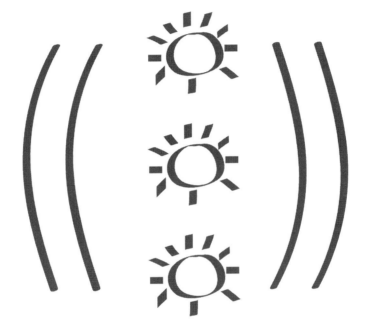

Tenth Dimension Angels

Eleventh Dimension Angels

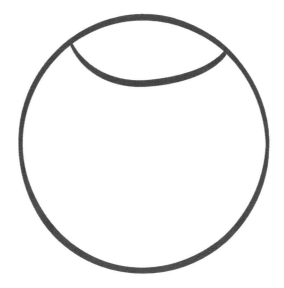

Twelfth Dimension Angels

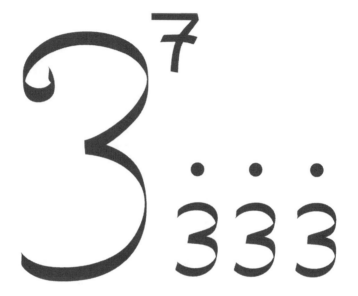

Sirius Angels

Pleiades Angels

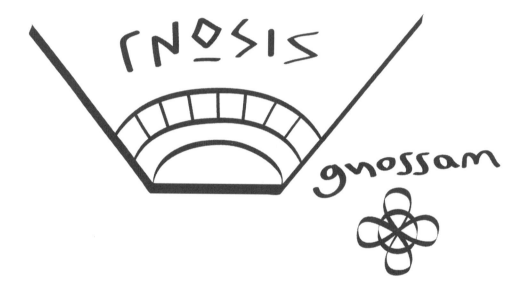

Shamballa Angels

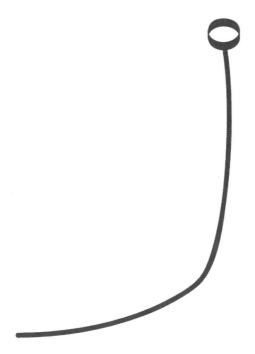

Dominion of Light

Unconditional Love

Blessings

Appendix

Angelic Hierarchy: The Angelic Order

Heaven is truly infinite. Reality surpasses and transcends any mind and imagination, its nature being infinite. Reality expands into infinity...It is Infinity...Infinitely Infinite, Infinite Infiniteness!

Similarly, there are countless Angels and celestial beings of great energy and light; beings of great Wisdom, great Power, and great Love; of great and of the Greatest, of high and of the Highest; of superior and of the Supreme Love, Power, Wisdom, Consciousness, Light, and Energy.

There are Angels for everything, for every single thing in Existence: Angels for anything immaterial and spiritual, and Angels for all things physical and material. Angels represent, express, manifest, guide, protect, compose, decompose, form, and reform everything that exists—anything spiritual or physical. Angels are one with God, and they are projections, emanations, energetic embodiments, vibratory expressions, and luminous creations of Divinity—that is, of the Whole and Absolute, of the Transcendent and Supreme, and of the Infinite and Eternal Reality, Source, Principle, and Power that is beyond all space, time, and matter, and beyond what is apparent and visible to the human eye or familiar and known to the human mind.

There is a substantial body of esoteric writings describing Angels and Archangels and their special names and qualities. Each Angel or Archangel performs a multiplicity of duties on Earth and throughout the universe. There are different Orders of Angels depending on the various duties, attributes, qualities, energies, or colors they radiate. It is natural that there are different experiences and point of views about Angels among various scholars, writers, mystics, and esoteric traditions, but there are also many similarities. Depending on the source in which Angels are mentioned, an Angel's name may be spelled in different ways, an Angel may have different qualities, or various Angels may be reported as having the same or similar attributes, qualities, and duties.

For example, Archangel Michael may be described as blue or azure flame/energy when Divine Power and Divine Will are perceived, but viewed as red flame/energy when protection, catharsis, and struggle against darkness and evil are at the forefront. Similarly, when Archangel Michael represents the Divine Consciousness, the Logos, and the Highest Wisdom, he is felt and perceived as a golden flame/energy. It must be understood that all the Angels and the Archangels are so much more than what we think, feel, see, or perceive them to be. It would not be wise to consider or anticipate that angelic beings will manifest merely as blue, green, or some other single color. These characteristics capture only aspects of their vast essences. Angels are not smaller, simpler, or less than humans, being truly amazing and magnificently complex multidimensional wonders of supreme divine art!

Angels encompass and contain all aspects, all colors, and all energies. However, we envision them as blue, red, golden, or green to attune ourselves mentally and spiritually to their luminous, divine energies. It is a process helpful for us human beings—a first, small, easy-to-follow, safe, steady, and stable step toward the Infinite!

What follows is a presentation of the Angelic Orders, the Angelic Hierarchy, and the celestial kingdom according to the relevant literature, esoteric teachings, and mystical experiences of great teachers. This presentation is a mere introduction to these wonderful celestial beings. Regular study of this material, and regular practice of relevant meditative and spiritual exercises, will enable you to tap into the Infinite Wisdom and Power of the heavens, discovering your own unique and special path to the Light.

The Angelic Hierarchy

The most universally accepted classification of the ranks of Angels is that of Pseudo-Dionysius the Areopagite, a philosopher of the fifth to sixth centuries AD; it was later adopted by Thomas Aquinas, whose life spanned between 1225–1274 AD. According to this angelic classification, celestial incorporeal spiritual beings are divided into definite Orders, each with different duties and separate frequencies and vibrations of energy. The Angelic Realm is divided into nine distinct Choirs or Orders of Angels within three major groups, known as Heavenly Spheres.

The nine Angelic Choirs or Orders are as follows:
- *Seraphim*
- *Cherubim*
- *Thrones or Ophanim*
- *Dominions*
- *Virtues*
- *Powers or Authorities*
- *Principalities or Rulers*
- *Archangels*
- *Angels*

Each Sphere contains three Orders or Choirs:

- *First Sphere (closest to the Divine): Seraphim, Cherubim, and Thrones or Ophanim*
- *Second Sphere: Dominions, Virtues, and Powers or Authorities*
- *Third Sphere (closest to Earth and humanity): Principalities or Rulers, Archangels, and Angels*

First Sphere:

Seraphim, Cherubim, Thrones

Seraphim

Seraphim comprise the highest Angelic Order and the closest Angels to God, in direct communication with Him. The name *Seraphim* means "the burning ones" or "the fiery ones." Their essence is of supreme divine fire, light, and love. The Seraphim, or Seraphs, are transcendent spiritual flames of Divine Love, and they are often referred to as "fiery serpents." They are represented by the serpent, symbol of healing. Their name possibly comes from *ser* (higher being) and *rapha* (healer).

They surround and protect God's Throne while continuously chanting the Trisagion— "Holy, Holy, Holy" and "Holy, Holy, Holy is the Lord of Hosts, the whole Earth is full of His Glory"—unceasingly praising the Divine. They protect the Divine Planes from evil and lower, negative vibrations. They were created with full knowledge and understanding of the Creator, and they move the heavens, as they emanate from the Divine.

The Seraphim encircle the throne of God and burn eternally with Love for the Creator. They establish and transmit the energy, the vibration, of Love. They are the supreme beings or Powers of Divine Love, as they emit and radiate the fiery light of God's Love to all worlds, all dimensions, all beings, and all the rest of the Angels. They are the Supreme Angels of Love, purifying humanity and inspiring us to perfect the internal flame of love and to move closer to the love of God.

Their transcendental light is so radiant that not even the members of the other Orders can look upon them, not even the Ophanim or the Cherubim; if human beings were to face them, we would be incinerated. However, Seraphim are also of such subtlety that they rarely are perceived by human consciousness; no being (human or angelic) can completely perceive or align with the Seraphim. They are the first and supreme emanation and creation of Divine Love, Power, and Wisdom, and they represent the full Glory, Grandeur, Miracles, and Splendor of the Divine Creative Source of All-That-Is.

According to the Third Book of Enoch (26:9–12), there are only four Seraphim, each one corresponding to the "four winds of the world." The Second Book of Enoch describes Seraphim as having four faces and six wings that correspond to the six days of creation. A Seraph covers its four faces with two of its wings, its feet with two others; with the remaining two wings, it flies. Each wing is the size of Heaven. Usually the Seraphim are depicted with the red color.

According to different texts and sources, the Seraphim Angels include Seraphiel ("Lord of Peace"), Michael, Metatron, Jehoel, Nathanael, and the fallen Angel Lucifer (known as Satan after his fall), who was the only Seraph with twelve wings. It is said that Satan, along with Sammael and Dubbiel, writes down on tablets the sins of humanity and then tells the Seraphim to transfer the tablets to God for humanity to be punished; however, the Seraphim know that God does not will this punishment, so they burn the tablets—symbolically, they purify, heal, and burn all of humanity's sins.

Cherubim

Cherubim comprise the second-highest Angelic Order after the Seraphim. They are the first Angels to be mentioned in the Old Testament (Genesis 3:22) and the ones mentioned most frequently in the Bible—as guardians of Eden and the Tree of Life, bearers of God's throne, or winged creatures of fire. According to Assyrian and Akkadian sources, their name means "fullness of God's knowledge," "one who prays," or "one who intercedes." Dionysius the Areopagite thought the word *Cherubim* denoted their power to know and behold God.

Cherubim are the Manifestations of Divine Wisdom and Knowledge. They are the keepers of the Knowledge of Heaven and of the Worlds, the voices of Divine Wisdom. They keep the *Book of Life*, the Akashic Records, which contain the details of all souls in the cosmos. Cherubim Angels manifest and guard Harmony; they are the Angels of stars, sun, and moon; and they act as guardians of stars and light.

Cherubim are depicted as four-winged beings having four faces—usually those of a man, ox, lion, and eagle. Their wings are joined one to another, so they can travel to any direction without having to turn. Their whole bodies and wings are covered with eyes, and they are associated with the color blue. Cherubim are also often depicted as huge, winged creatures with the faces of humans and the bodies of eagles or sphinxes, resembling Egyptian sphinxes. The Bible describes the upper lid (Mercy Seat) on the Ark of the Covenant as being adorned with golden Cherubim whose wings stretched over the Mercy Seat. When Adam and Eve were expelled from the Garden of Eden, God assigned Cherubim and a flaming sword to guard the Garden of Eden and the way to the Tree of Life.

Cherubim are often confused with putti, the baby Angels depicted especially in Renaissance art holding golden trumpets.

Cherubim are considered to be beings of ultimate protection. They guide humanity through the Tree of Life back to the Garden of Eden and the Throne of God (the Divine Source).

Chief Cherubim Angels include Cherubiel, Ophaniel, Zophiel, Raphael, and Gabriel.

Thrones (or Ophanim)

Thrones are also known as Ophanim or Erelim. They stand under God's Throne, hence their name. The Hebrew word *Ophanim* means "wheels" or "spheres." They have the most unusual appearances of any celestial beings: big fiery wheels with hundreds of eyes. They are Higher and Holy Spirits of Divine Wisdom and Divine Will. They make known the Will of God and manifest His Decisions. They are also Angels of Divine

Justice. Their mission is to inspire faith in the power of God and bestow Divine Justice. They manifest Peace, Objectivity, and Humbleness.

Thrones are assigned to guard the planets. Thrones are also closely connected to the Cherubim because they travel together; they are the actual wheels beneath the *Merkabah* (the chariot-throne of God) driven by the Cherubim. Thrones, along with the Seraphim and Cherubim, never sleep but always guard the throne of God.

Chief Angels of this Order include Oriphiel, Zaphkiel, Zadkiel, and Raziel.

Second Sphere:

Dominions, Virtues, Powers

Dominions

The Dominions get their name from *dominatus*, the Latin word for "domination," and from a translation of the Greek word *kyriotites*, meaning "lordships." In Hebrew they are also known as *Hashmallim*, and it is through them that God's majesty is revealed. They are ministers of God's justice to the cosmos. They manifest spirit in physical form; their purpose is to integrate the spiritual and material worlds. Each Dominion is perceived to be carrying a scepter and a golden rod or the seal of God. They are Divinely Beautiful. They are assigned to teach and oversee the duties and activities of all other Angels and to maintain cosmic order. Dominions preside over Nations, and they rarely appear to human beings. They also govern the natural world and the elements. It is said that Hashmal and Zadkiel are among the Dominions.

Virtues

Virtues are called "the shining ones" because they radiate the most luminous light. They govern the sun, stars, planets, moon, and galaxies to maintain harmony and order in the cosmos. On Earth they oversee the seasons and every facet of natural life. Their purpose is to transfer spiritual energy to the earthly plane and the collective human consciousness. They are the Angels that work great miracles since they are able to surpass the laws of nature. They are Angels of Divine Grace and Divine Mercy; they bestow grace and valor within the human heart. They are closely connected to saints, and they offer them the ability to work healing miracles. The two Angels present at

Jesus Christ's Ascension and the ones comforting him before his crucifixion were from the Order of Virtues. Members of the Order of Virtues include Michael, Raphael, Barbiel, Usiel, Peliel, and Haniel.

Powers (Authorities)

Powers have been credited as being the very first Angels created by God. They are guardians of cosmic order and peace, and they constantly fight evil. They have been assigned to record human history and to be present during the births and deaths of all humans. The Powers include the mighty Lords of Karma (Karmic Angels) and the Angels of birth and death. The Karmic Angels keep the collective history of humanity and planet Earth; they also guard and maintain the Akashic Records (database of all souls and their journeys). They constantly protect the world from being taken over by demons and evil. They guard the path to the celestial realms and maintain the border between Heaven and Earth. Powers protect souls from evil; it is believed that when we die, these Angels guide our safe transitions to the celestial realms. They assist each soul to overcome temptations, and they give strength to people. It is said that Samael and Camael belong to the Order of Powers.

Third Sphere:

Principalities, Archangels, Angels

Principalities (Rulers)

Principalities collaborate with Powers in issues of authority and power. Their symbols include the scepter, the cross, and the sword. Principalities are the guardians and protectors of such large groups as nations, countries, cities, towns, and organizations. They have a direct impact on the affairs of humanity, and they inspire ideas. They protect science and art and also have religion and politics under their care. They teach and empower groups and people, they are rulers of time, and they manifest higher divine blessings in the physical world. Members of this Order include Aniel and Camael.

Archangels

Archangels, sometimes referred to as *Archangeloi*, are Angels of High Order, the most important mediators between humanity and the Divine. The word *Archangel* means "chief or leading Angel." They are the better-known celestial beings that act on various levels, realms, and dimensions. They carry messages of the Divine to people and carry out the Divine Will. They emit the Infinite Love, Wisdom, and Power of the Divine Creator. They represent, express, and manifest Divine Energies, Aspects, and Qualities, and also the Elements of Nature. Archangels oversee and guide the Angelic Orders, which include countless benevolent and pure celestial beings of Divine Light and Divine Love. They also oversee the Guardian Angels. Archangel Michael, Archangel Gabriel, and Archangel Raphael are the most-known Archangels. They have been the closest to humanity, guiding our multidimensional, spiritual, and earthly paths of advancement to higher states of consciousness, light, love, wisdom, wholeness, and oneness.

Michael and Gabriel are the only Archangels mentioned in the Bible. Raphael is mentioned in the Book of Tobit and Uriel in the apocryphal Book of Enoch. Archangels Michael, Gabriel, and Raphael are venerated in the Roman Catholic Church on September 29 and in the Orthodox Church on November 8.

Islam recognizes the existence of four Archangels: Mikhail (Michael, Angel of Mercy), Jibril, (Gabriel, responsible for revealing the Quran to Muhammad and communicating with the prophets), Israfil (Raphael, responsible for signaling the coming of Judgment Day) and Azrael (Angel of Death, responsible for parting the soul from the human body).

Zoroastrianism (founded in the sixth century BC) was formerly among the most primal and important monotheistic religions (most probably the first monotheistic religion), and possibly the first to mention Angels. It had a profound influence on the three largest monotheistic religions of today: Judaism, Christianity, and Islam. Zoroastrianism passed on several parables, philosophical and moral principles, and other elements to these three large religions, among them the distinction between good and evil and the battle between good and evil. In Zoroastrianism, the Sublime Force is Ahura Mazda, who created six Archangels called the *Amesha Spentas* (meaning "Bounteous Immortal") that represent aspects of the Divine (the noncreated Creator). *Amesha Spentas* are Emanations and Divine Sparks of the Creator, Ahura Mazda. Those are perhaps the earliest references to Archangels. In addition, Zoroastrianism mentions Fravashi, the guardian spirits or Guardian Angels that all people have.

There are respective references to Archangels in Eastern religions and philosophies: Buddhist tradition has *Devas* (celestial beings) and *Dharmapalas* (Karma protectors), while Hinduism has *Devas* and *Mahadevas*.

It is highly intriguing, from a philosophical and metaphysical point of view, that Lucifer—whose name means "light bearer," but who is also known as Satan, which means "the opposer, the adversary" in Hebrew—was initially an Archangel! Lucifer was the most beautiful and luminous Archangel. Then he exalted himself against God and fell from grace. Archangel Michael was the one that led the battle against Lucifer and succeeded in casting him out of Heaven, along with the Angels who had chosen to follow him. This parable has many layers; one can reflect upon the correspondence of this parable to the course of man on Earth and his life in the material world.

The Archangels are countless. The most-known Archangels to be assigned and devoted to humanity include Michael, Gabriel, Raphael, Uriel, Haniel, Jophiel, Zadkiel, Tzaphkiel, Chamuel, Raguel, Raziel, Ariel, Jeremiel, Samael, Azrael, Sandalphon, and Metatron.

Archangel Michael

The most-known Angel of Heaven is Archangel Michael, who is as close as it gets to the Divine and also to humanity. He is the most prominent Angel in Christian, Jewish, and Islamic lore. His name means "who is as God," and he protects and guides all humanity. Archangel Michael is the Power of God (Divine Source and Reality) manifested in form and action. According to Stylianos Atteshlis (known as Daskalos), *Michael* comes from *maha* (meaning "great" in Sanskrit) and *el* (meaning "God" in Sanskrit, Ancient Egyptian, and Hebrew).

Archangel Michael fights and defeats the evil; he is the Light that negates darkness. He is the Archangel of Protection and Purification, of the Divine Guidance and Will. His element is Fire, and usually he is depicted holding a sword. He is considered to be the leader of the Archangels and the Order of Virtues; he is called the prince or lord or commander of the heavenly host, the master of all Angels. Michael is one of the Seven Archangels of the Throne (the highest ranks in the Order of the Archangels) and also the Angel of Presence, Justice, and Mercy. He is the keeper of the Keys of Heaven, ruler of the Fourth Heaven, and, according to various sources, a ruler of the Seventh Heaven as well. Michael's mystical name is Sabbathiel, his ancient Persian name is Beshter, and he is also called the Prince of Light.

Michael is the Chief Warrior fighting Evil and Satan, the Archangel of battle and defender of Heaven. In the War in Heaven, he cast Lucifer (Satan) out of Heaven after defeating him. Michael is referred to as the Angel of Death, for he takes the souls of the dead to the afterlife, leading them to Heaven. Michael taught Adam how to farm and care for his family after being expelled from the Garden of Eden and persuaded God to allow Adam's soul to return to Heaven after he died.

Orthodox Christians refer to him as Taxiarch Archangel Michael, and Roman Catholics as Saint Michael the Archangel. Perhaps Archangel Michael is the highest, most direct, and best-known manifestation of the Divine on Earth.

In the Tree of Life, Archangel Michael presides over Hod, the eighth Sephirah.

Archangel Gabriel

Archangel Gabriel, the second-most-known Angel of Heaven, is second in rank only to Archangel Michael. Gabriel's name means "God is my strength." According to Stylianos Atteshlis, *Gabriel* (Ka-Vir-El) means "Divine Soul Element" because *ka* is "soul" in Ancient Egyptian, *vir* is "element" in Ancient Egyptian, and *el* is "God" in Sanskrit, Ancient Egyptian, and Hebrew.

Gabriel is the Archangel of the Water Element, of the Soul, of Emotions, of Serenity, of Love, of Joy, and of Divine Grace. He is considered to be the Angel of Sleep and of the Fourth Dimension. He is the Divine Messenger. He is the one who announced to Mary that she would be the mother of Jesus Christ and to Elizabeth that she would be the mother of John the Baptist. He is also the Angel of Annunciation, of Resurrection, of Mercy, and of the Revelation (he will blow the trumpet to signal the Judgment Day). In Judaic lore, Gabriel is believed to be a female Archangel. Gabriel has been accredited as the Angel who instructs the newly incarnating souls to be birthed into the material world. The entirety of his collective roles is quite complex. He is regarded as the Angel of First Heaven and the one who sits on the left hand of God. He is the Angel of Justice and Truth.

Archangel Gabriel presides over Yesod, the ninth Sephirah in the Tree of Life.

Archangel Raphael

Archangel Raphael is one of the highest-ranking Archangels, and he is known as the Angel of Healing. He has in his care the healing of Earth and of humanity. His name means "God heals." According to Stylianos Atteshlis, *Raphael* (Ra-Fa-El) means "God of the Vital Power and Energy of the Sun" because *ra* is "sun" in Ancient Egyptian, *fa* is "vibration and energy" in Ancient Egyptian, and *el* is "God" in Sanskrit, Ancient Egyptian, and Hebrew.

Raphael is the Archangel of Etheric Vitality, of Life-Force Energy, of Healing, of Medicine, and of all Sciences, and the Angel of the Sun. He is known to be the ruling prince of the Second Heaven and guardian of the Tree of Life in Eden. He is one of the Seven Archangels of the Throne (the highest rank in the Order of the Archangels) and also the Angel of Presence. He is the Archangel connected to the elements of Ether and Air.

Archangel Raphael presides over Tiphareth, the sixth Sephirah in the Tree of Life.

Archangel Uriel

Uriel links humanity to the spiritual realms and to the understanding of the Divine. His name means "Light of God" or "Fire of God," and he is the most radiant of all Angels. According to Stylianos Atteshlis, *Uriel* (U-Ra-El) means "God of Light and of Earth, of the Material Plane" as the letter *U* means "space and matter" in Ancient Egyptian, *ra* means "sun" in Ancient Egyptian, and *el* means "God" in Sanskrit, Ancient Egyptian, and Hebrew.

Uriel is the Archangel of Balance and Harmony; he keeps in balance all Elements and all Bodies of Man. As the Angel of Repentance, he helps us to understand the universal laws of Karma. He is the Archangel of Manifestation and Grounding, the Great Harmonizer of All. Uriel is the Angel of Mental Clarity and also the Angel of Music, the Heavenly Melodies, and the Music of the Spheres. He is also called Angel of the Sun, Angel of Presence, Angel of Salvation, interpreter of prophecies, Seraph, or Cherub. He is also equated with Phanuel, and he is the guardian of planet Mars.

He is considered to stand at the gate of the Garden of Eden with his flaming sword.

Uriel is connected to the weather elements of thunder and lightning and to the Element of Earth.

Archangel Sandalphon

Archangel Sandalphon is responsible for carrying the prayers of people to the Divine Source. He is said to have been incarnated on Earth as the prophet Elijah and to have become an Archangel after his Ascension to Heaven.

Sandalphon's name may be derived from Greek, meaning "co-brother," a possible reference to his twin brother Archangel Metatron, who was also once incarnated, as the wise scribe Enoch. They are the only two Archangels whose name doesn't end in *-el,* which means "God" in Sanskrit, Ancient Egyptian, and Hebrew.

Sandalphon is the Archangel of Nature and of Earth, bringing harmony to the nature elements. He is the Archangel of Balance and Harmony; we invoke Sandalphon to help us with grounding and healing of the Earth. He is also associated with music and all forms of music therapy, while being also a patron Angel of Music and Heavenly Song.

Sandalphon is considered to be a Sarim Angel (i.e., an Angelic Prince), Angel of Prayer, Angel of Tears, and Fighter of Evil, similar to Archangel Michael. He is the one responsible for deciding the gender of a baby. He is said to be the tallest of all Angels and ruler of the Seventh Heaven.

Archangel Sandalphon presides over Malkuth, the tenth Sephirah in the Tree of Life.

Archangel Metatron

Archangel Metatron is responsible for recording everything that happens upon Earth, keeping the Akashic Records or *Book of Life.* His name has various possible etymologies. Metatron is made up of two Greek words, *meta* and *thronos,* which combined together mean "the one who stands next to or before the throne of God." He is called Prince of the Divine Face, Angel of Presence, and Chancellor of Heaven. Metatron is the only Archangel (except his brother, Archangel Sandalphon) within the angelic realm who was once human before becoming Archangel. His name doesn't end in *-el,* which means "God" in Sanskrit, Ancient Egyptian, and Hebrew. On Earth, Metatron was known as Enoch, a prophet and a wise scribe, the seventh patriarch after Adam. Enoch ascended to Heaven and transformed into Archangel Metatron.

Metatron might be the greatest Archangel of all; he is called the King of Angels. He is the Archangel of Enlightenment and Ascension. He has in his care the sustenance of human life and acts as a direct link between the Divine Source and humanity. Metatron receives daily orders from God regarding the souls to be taken that day, and he transmits them to Gabriel and Samael; he is the Supreme Angel of Death. He is the Archangel of Platinum Energy and Ray and Keeper of the Inner and Outer Light of God. Metatron has been credited with such majesty and Power that he is even referred to as Lesser YHWH, that is, the lesser God. He possesses seventy-two other names as well.

Metatron is said to be the tallest Angel in the Angelic Hierarchy and also the youngest one. He resides in the Seventh Heaven, where he records all heavenly and earthly events.

Archangel Metatron presides over Kether, the first Sephirah in the Tree of Life.

Archangel Haniel (Anael, Aniel)

Haniel is the Archangel of Joy. His name means "Grace of God" or "Joy of God." He is one of the chief Angels in charge of the Angelic Order of Principalities, and he takes care of all nations on Earth. Haniel is the Archangel of Grace, of Healing, and of Natural Intuitive and Psychic Abilities. His presence facilitates Emotional Communication and Divine Communication.

Haniel is also said to have escorted the scribe Enoch to the spiritual realm before he became Archangel Metatron. Haniel rules the planet Venus. He is listed as one of the seven Archangels of the Divine Throne. He collaborates on various tasks with Archangel Metatron.

Archangel Haniel presides over Netzach, the seventh Sephirah in the Tree of Life.

Archangel Chamuel (Camael, Khamael, Camiel)

Archangel Chamuel embodies the principle of unconditional pure love. His name means "He who seeks God" or "He who sees God." He is the Archangel of Divine Love and Human Relationships; he works on bringing love to all people. He is considered to be the patron Angel of people going through rough times in relationships and people working for world peace. Chamuel is the chief of the Angelic Order of Powers and one of the Seven Archangels of the Divine Throne. He is said to have comforted Jesus in the garden of Gethsemane on the night before his arrest. He is associated with the planet Mars. Chamuel represents the qualities of Love, Tolerance, and Gratitude. He offers Courage, Patience, and Strength.

Archangel Chamael presides over Geburah, the fifth Sephirah in the Tree of Life.

Archangel Raziel

Archangel Raziel is the Keeper of Universal Secrets and the Angel of Mysteries. His name means "Secrets of God." He is the possessor of all celestial and earthly knowledge. He reveals holy secrets only when the Divine Source allows him to do so.

Raziel stands so close to God that he hears and writes down everything God says, and then he writes God's secret insights about the entire universe. Raziel is credited with writing the *Book of Raziel the Angel*, a book where in all divine secrets about celestial and earthly knowledge are set down. Raziel gave the book to Adam and Eve after they were expelled from Eden, so they could better understand God and find their way back home to Eden.

According to various teachings, Raziel is the chief Angel of Erelim and an Archangel of metaphysical teachings.

Archangel Raziel presides over Chokmah, the second Sephirah in the Tree of Life.

Archangel Ariel

Archangel Ariel is aligned with the Natural World, Air, Water, Nature Spirits (Elementals), and Animals. His name means "Lion of God." Ariel is associated with cleansing and purifying the Earth; he is often called the Guardian and Lord of the Earth. He oversees the protection and healing of wild and domestic animals and of Earth's elements. He is the Archangel of Environment and Wild Animals, ruler of Earth and its elements.

Ariel, as a Healer Archangel, works with Archangel Raphael in the healing arts, and, as a Protector Archangel, he works with Archangel Michael. Sometimes he is associated with Archangel Uriel.

Archangel Tzaphkiel

Archangel Tzaphkiel is known as the Angel of understanding and compassion. His name has various meanings, such as "Contemplation of God" and "Knowledge of God." Tzaphkiel embodies the feminine aspect of Creation, and he is considered the Archangel of Higher Love and Maternal Love. According to Jewish tradition, he belongs to the Angelic Order of Erelim. Tzaphkiel is called the Watchtower of God because he observes God's Love and passes it along to humanity. He is the Archangel of Divine Contemplation, of Universal Insight and Lucidity, and of Connection to Angelic and Spiritual Realms.

Archangel Tzaphkiel presides over Binah, the third Sephirah in the Tree of Life.

Archangel Zadkiel

Archangel Zadkiel is the Archangel of Mercy, Freedom, Justice, and Forgiveness. His name means "Righteousness of God" and "Justice of God." He embodies the spirit of the Divine Violet Ray (the Seventh Ray), and he is the Archangel of Transmutation, of Benevolence, of Healing, and of Purification.

According to Kabbalah, Zadkiel is one of the two Archangels (the other is Jophiel) who assist and follow directly behind Archangel Michael when he fights evil. Zadkiel is considered to be the unnamed Angel who stopped Abraham from killing his son, Isaac, as a sacrifice to God. He is also an Angel who presides over matters such as prosperity and forgiveness; he is often associated with helping women during pregnancy and birth. He is one of the Seven Archangels of the Divine Throne, and he is chief of the Angelic Order of Dominions (in Jewish tradition equated with the Order of *Hashmallim*). Zadkiel rules the planet Jupiter.

Zadkiel is known as the Divine Alchemist and Angelic Lord of the Violet Flame of Alchemical Transformation. He works with Ascended Master St. Germain as guardian of the Violet Flame. The workings of the Seventh Ray (violet ray) focus on purifying and transmuting the lower energies of human beings into more evolved energies and spiritual states at all levels of being. Zadkiel teaches us the use of violet flame and helps us to heal the human mind, body, soul, and aura. The violet flame and energy of Archangel Zadkiel offers protection, strength, and spiritual guidance.

Archangel Zadkiel presides over Chesed, the fourth Sephirah in the Tree of Life.

Archangel Jophiel

Archangel Jophiel is the Archangel of Beauty and Art, the patron Angel of artists and intellectuals. His name means "Beauty of God." It is Jophiel's duty to transmit Divine Inspiration into the minds of people and help them co-create beauty and art on Earth. He is the chief of the Angelic Order of Seraphim, and he assists Archangel Michael in battle. He is said to work closely with Archangel Metatron. Jewish tradition considers Jophiel as the Angel who guarded the Tree of Knowledge and drove Adam and Eve away from the Garden of Eden.

Jophiel serves on the Second Ray of Love and Wisdom. He is the Archangel of Wisdom, Knowledge, and Illumination.

Archangel Jeremiel

Archangel Jeremiel is the Archangel of Clairvoyance, Prophecy, Intuition, and Dreams. In Judaic tradition, Jeremiel is listed as one of the seven core Archangels. His name means "Mercy of God." Jeremiel helps the souls newly crossed over into Heaven to review their earthly lives and learn from their experiences. He also guards the knowledge of the exact day of the final judgment.

Archangel Samael

According to Christian mystic Stylianos Atteshlis (known as "Daskalos"), the name of Samael comes from *sam*, which means "venom," and *el*, which means "God" in Sanskrit, Ancient Egyptian, and Hebrew. In Kabbalistic texts, Samael is described as the "Severity of God," and in Gnostic texts his name stands for "the Blind God."

Archangel Samael is one of the Angels of Death (together with Azrael). He symbolizes and manifests darkness and the negative aspect but also healing and enlightenment. He has been regarded as both a good and an evil Angel. In esoteric and spiritual healing arts, Samael is considered to be an Angel of post-death soul liberation, of transitions to other levels, and of change generally. He is also the Angel of healing many internal issues, including the damaged human subconscious, the "shadow" side (lower self, flaws), any negative feelings and thoughts, and all deeply rooted, unconscious fears.

Samael performs the Will of God and dispenses Divine Justice. He is regarded as a punisher and great defender at the same time. In Kabbalistic tradition, Samael is related with planet Mars and the Sephirah Geburah (meaning "severity"), which is the domain of justice, punishment, and security.

Samael is an Angel of matter (in its dense form). In cooperation with the four Archangels (Michael, Gabriel, Raphael, Uriel) and the Four Elements (Fire, Water, Air, Earth), Samael—as the Angel of Earth and minerals—directly controls matter and can materialize and dematerialize. He creates dense matter (providing us with the materials for bones, muscles, and organs of the body) under the watch of natural and Karmic laws. Samael has a prominent role in the maintenance of physical health. He materializes all the thoughts, ideas, and desires of the human soul through the four bodies: spirit, mind, emotion, and matter. Working with Samael may bring about the more intense and direct (possibly miraculous) healing that requires any alteration of matter, such as materialization or dematerialization.

A direct collaboration with Samael can be achieved only by advanced mystics who have been unified or "egofied" (i.e., attuned to the highest level) with the four Archangels of the four Elements, after a long, deep esoteric practice in the art of meditation and visualization.

Samael resides in the Seventh Heaven and helps us to overcome our fear of death.

Archangel Azrael

Archangel Azrael is known as the Angel of Death in both Islamic and Jewish traditions. His name means "whom God helps." In Islam, Azrael is the Angel of Death who separates the human soul from the body at the moment of death and keeps track of the dying by erasing their names. In various sources, he is described as a fallen Angel. Although associated with being the Angel of Death, he is a gentle and comforting Archangel who assists people with grieving. Azrael's Angelic duties include comforting people prior to their physical deaths and helping souls depart from the physical realm and transition to the spiritual realm.

Azrael works in the area of esoteric and spiritual healing arts. He is considered to be an Angel of Post-Death Soul Liberation, of Transitions to other levels, and of Change generally. Just like Samael, he is also the Angel of healing the human subconscious, the "shadow" side, negative feelings and thoughts, and deeply rooted unconscious fears. Azrael helps us to see what is true and substantial. He rules the planet Pluto, and he is often associated with water and the flow of life.

Archangel Raguel

Archangel Raguel is the Archangel of Justice and Fairness. The Book of Enoch regards Raguel as one of the Seven Archangels who judge those who disrespect God's laws. His name means "friend of God." Raguel oversees the entire angelic realm and all creation to make sure that they all (Angels and humans) work together in a harmonious way according to the Divine Order and Will. He is a leader within the Angelic Order of Principalities and the Archangel of Friendship, Cooperation, Balance, and Orderliness.

Characteristics of Archangels

Below you will find a list with the qualities and characteristics of each Archangel, including their resonance with colors and energies.

The Domains of the Archangels

Michael: Protection, Guidance, Purification, Divine Will
Gabriel: Feelings, Serenity, Peace, Hope, Regeneration
Raphael: Healing
Uriel: Light, Grounding, Balance, Harmony
Sandalphon: Nature, Grounding, Balance, Harmony
Metatron: Enlightenment, Ascension
Haniel: Joy, Psychic Abilities, Emotional Communication
Chamuel: Love, Relationships
Raziel: Rite, Mysteries, Knowledge and Wisdom of the Universe
Ariel: Environment, Wild Nature, Water, Wind
Tzaphkiel: Maternal Energy and Love, Reflection, Angelic Realms
Zadkiel: Justice, Compassion, Forgiveness, Purification, Healing
Jophiel: Beauty, Art, Knowledge, Wisdom
Jeremiel: Compassion, Insight, Prophecy, Dreams
Samael: Transition, Change, Deep Healing, Materialization and Dematerialization
Azrael: Transition, Change, Healing of Subconscious
Raguel: Friendship, Cooperation, Justice, Harmony

The Colors and Energies of the Archangels

Michael: Red (Fire, Purification, Protection) or Blue/Azure (Divine Will) or Gold (Divine Protection and Power)

Gabriel: Blue/Azure (Water, Feelings, Serenity) or Fuchsia (Divine Love, Care, Maternal Energy) or White (Purity)

Raphael: Green/Emerald Green (Body Healing) or Purple/Violet (Etheric Vitality, Life-Force Energy) or White (Light of Life)

Uriel: White or Silver

Sandalphon: Green, Stone/Earthly Colors

Metatron: Platinum

Haniel: Azure, Baby Blue

Chamuel: Pink

Raziel: Deep Blue

Ariel: Pale Green

Tzaphkiel: Turquoise

Zadkiel: Violet

Jophiel: Yellow

Jeremiel: Violet

Samael: Deep Green

Azrael: Deep Red

Raguel: Orange, Yellow

Guardian Angel: All colors (rainbow) or White (purity) or Pink (selfless maternal love and care) or Azure (celestial serenity and protection)

Angels

Angels are substantial spiritual beings, true heavenly creatures. They are immaterial beings of pure consciousness who carry out divine purposes and acts. One of their duties is to transfer messages from human beings to the Higher Power, God (the Ultimate Sublime Reality and Source of everything) and vice versa. Angels are most known to people as messengers of the Divine, and their name comes from the Greek word *angelos*, which means "messenger." Nevertheless, Angels have countless duties and tasks, attributes and characteristics, qualities and powers: encouraging direct communication between human beings and the Divine and transferring messages, ideas, inspirations, heavenly guidance, spiritual energies, and qualities.

There are countless Angels for every area of life and for everything: Angels of harmony, peace, freedom, faith, joy, mercy, compassion, power, knowledge, beauty, and so on; Angels of arts, sciences, colors, sounds, music; Angels of nature, water, air, earth, rivers, animals, rocks, minerals, and many others. There are also Guardian Angels, Angels of protection, Angels of healing, Angels of purification, Angels of guidance, Angels of illumination, Angels of abundance, and Angels of love, romance, family, and all relationships. Angels guide each person individually. They are our heavenly siblings!

Two distinct and special Angelic Orders

There are celestial beings of superior angelic energy and power that are not part of the known nine Orders of the Angelic Hierarchy. These are spiritual entities of the highest light, such as Elohim and Shekhinah. There is not much information available about these primordial and transcendental cosmic forces because humanity cannot attune with such high levels of consciousness and being.

Elohim

The Elohim are Sons of God. They are not part of the known Angelic Hierarchy; they are viewed by esoteric traditions and sources as higher spiritual entities of Divine consciousness and infinite light. It is believed that seven or twelve Elohim exist. They are the primary essence of the Creator in form; they are makers of dimensions, universes, and worlds. Elohim are the hands and creative forces of God. They are emanations of the Divine Source that serve as the Highest Angelic Creators. They might be connected with other ancient systems of twelve deities or forces, such as the twelve Olympians. In the Old Testament, the Hebrew word Elohim is commonly used to refer to God.

Shekhinah

Shekhinah is a mystical embodiment of the feminine aspect of God—the Feminine Principle of Existence and the Infinite Divine Being. She is also called the bride of God. She is the Divine Source's hidden presence made manifest. In Kabbalah, the Shekhinah is the archetype of the Divine female, and she is represented as Sephirah Malkut, "the daughter of God." She is also symbolized by the moon, which reflects the light of the sun. Shekhinah is the Divine Presence, the Divine Source of Life, the Divine Mother. She is the female counterpart of Archangel Metatron. Shekhinah is the connection from

Earth to Heaven, and Metatron is the connection from Heaven to Earth. Shekhinah and Metatron are different aspects of the Divine. The Gnostics say she is Pistis Sophia. Shekhinah is believed to be the Mother of Angels.

Guardian Angel

The Guardian Angel belongs to the Order of Angels. Stylianos Atteshlis (known as "Daskalos") taught that the Guardian Angel belongs to the Order of Thrones. The Guardian Angel is the most important Angel and the one closest to us, the most immediate, direct, and personal—the most loving and beloved—among all celestial spiritual beings.

Each Guardian Angel is connected directly to the soul and the personality of one person. Every soul has a Guardian Angel assigned and attuned to it for its protection and guidance. A Guardian Angel is a divine blueprint, an angelic "duplicate" of a human being's soul. A Guardian Angel is a person's celestial "other half."

Each human being has a Guardian Angel assigned by God to watch over him. The Guardian Angel assigned to each person is unique, though it is possible to connect to more Guardian Angels as we advance and evolve spiritually. A Guardian Angel accompanies, protects, supports, and guides a person through his entire life; listens to his prayers, comforts him; loves him deeply, wholly, totally, and unconditionally. He is love in its most angelic form, the angelic aspect of our Higher Selves. A person and his Guardian Angel are spiritually united, eternal beings existing in the bliss and completeness of the Divine Source.

The Guardian Angel cannot bypass our free will to reach greater maturation and self-discovery through the various separations, conflicts, and sorrows we experience in our lives. Guardian Angels minister to human beings (souls on Earth) as our guides and protectors, always according to the wishes of our higher selves—the intentions, choices, and plans of our wise souls. The Guardian Angels appear at our rescue only when that action is in accordance with the deepest wishes of our souls and with the karmic laws. They will not stop us from learning the hard way what we have chosen to learn, but they will rescue us if we are in danger and it is not our time to die. Our Guardian Angels will guide us to places, directions, or people we are supposed to find, necessary for our development. They will inspire us and answer our questions, once we are ready and open to higher truths.

As we lovingly call upon our Guardian Angels (even by just thinking of them), we connect with them energetically and build a relationship that helps us advance in our spiritual and everyday lives. The greatest wish of each Guardian Angel is to help us grow and stay on the path of harmony.

The Guardian Angel is the most precious gift from Heaven, from the Divine Source, from God to humanity, to each one of us. That great, unique, personal, close, and intimate gift is the love of Heaven and of Spirit—the Divine Love!

Summary Tables of Angelic Symbols

Angelic Love

Angelic Light

Angelic Guidance

Angelic Abundance

Angelic Serenity

Angelic Protection

Angelic Joy

Angelic Healing

Angelic Peace

Angelic Justice

Angelic Mercy

Angelic Dominion

Angelic Relaxation

Angelic Energy

Angelic Dream

Angelic Sleep

Angelic Prediction

Angelic Grace

Angelic Freedom

Angelic Truth

Angelic
Expression-Communication

Angelic Perfection

Angelic Principles

Angelic Laws

Angelic Scripts

Angelic Flow

Angelic Structures

Angelic Mathematics

Angelic Insight

Angelic Intuition

Angelic Detoxification

Angelic Body

Angelic Health

Angelic Miracle

Angelic Speech

Angelic Art

Angelic Knowledge

Angelic Awakening

Angelic Particles

Angelic Matter

Angelic Colors

Angelic Sound

Angelic Rays

Angelic Spheres

Angelic Pyramid

Angelic Music

Angelic Dance

Angelic Flying

Angelic Elevation

Angelic Beauty

Angelic Life

Angelic Happiness

Angelic Good Fortune

Angelic Wealth

Angelic Friendship

Angelic Romance

Angelic Work

Angelic Purpose

Angelic Adaptation

Angelic House

Angelic Spiritual Powers

Angelic Talents

Angelic Consciousness

Angelic Unity

Angelic Ecstasy

Angelic Forgiveness

Angelic Repentance

Angelic Expansion

Angelic Completion

Angelic Blessing

Angelic Wisdom

Angelic Power

Angelic Past

Angelic Future

Angelic Present

Angelic Time

Angelic Play and Playfulness

Angelic Resting
and Rejuvenation

Angelic Satisfaction

Angelic Fullness

Angelic Courage

Angelic Hope

Angelic Brotherhood
and Sisterhood

Angelic Deep Healing

Angelic Kindness

Angelic Compassion

Angelic Togetherness

Angelic Aura

Angelic Aura Healing

Angelic Emotional Healing

Angelic Mental Healing

Angelic Spiritual Healing

Angelic Cellular Healing

Angelic DNA

Angelic Healing
of the 1st Chakra

Angelic Healing
of the 2nd Chakra

Angelic Healing
of the 3rd Chakra

Angelic Healing
of the 4th Chakra

Angelic Healing
of the 5th Chakra

Angelic Healing
of the 6th Chakra

Angelic Healing
of the 7th Chakra

Angelic Healing
of the Soul Chakra

Angelic Healing
of the Earth Chakra

Angelic Relationship Healing

Angelic Healing of Life,
Direction, Purpose

Angelic Karma Healing

Angelic Clearing
of Negative Influence

Angelic Purification
of Negative Energy

Angelic Easiness

Angelic Transcendence

Angelic Inspiration

Angelic Answers

Angelic Message

Angelic Manners

Angelic Rehabilitation

Angelic Order and Organization

Angelic Study and Learning

Angelic Providence

Angelic Help

Angelic Realm,
Level, Dimension

Angelic Heavenly
Stairway / Bridge

Angelic Thought

Angelic Emotion

Angelic Spirit

Angelic Soul

Angelic Creativity

Angelic Child

Angelic Centre

Angelic Enlightenment

Angelic Ascension

Angelic Release

Angelic Cleansing

Angelic Purity

Angelic Relationships

Angelic Character

Angelic Intention

Angelic Focus

Angelic Priority

Angelic Earth

Angelic Water

Angelic Fire

Angelic Air

Angelic Baptism

Angelic Painkiller

Angelic Planetary
Enlightenment

Angelic Planetary Healing

Angelic Repairing

Angelic Recreation
and Reconstruction

Angelic Invention

Angelic Memory

Angelic Endurance

Angelic Courage

Angelic Optimism

Angelic Empowerment

Angelic Initiation

Angelic Attunement

Angelic Harmonization

Angelic Harmony

Angelic Balance

Angelic Healing Powers

Angelic Self-Healing

Angelic Family

Angelic Connection

Angelic Meditation

Angelic Faith

Angelic Trust

Angelic Honesty

Angelic Warmth

Angelic Gratitude

Angelic Secrets

Angelic Sacredness

Angelic Holiness

Angelic Openness

Angelic Acceptance

Angelic Activation

Angelic Lessons

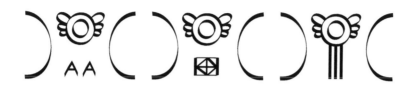 

| Angelic Codes | Angelic Grounding | Angelic Manifestation and Materialization | Seraphim |

| Cherubim | Thrones (Ophanim) | Dominions | Virtues |

| Powers (Authorities) | Principalities (Rulers) | Archangels | Angels |

| Archangel Michael | Archangel Gabriel | Archangel Raphael | Archangel Uriel |

Archangel Sandalphon

Archangel Metatron

Archangel Haniel

Archangel Chamuel (Camael)

Archangel Raziel

Archangel Ariel

Archangel Tzaphkiel

Archangel Zadkiel

Archangel Jophiel

Archangel Jeremiel

Archangel Samael

Archangel Azrael

Archangel Raguel

Guardian Angel

Shekhinah

Elohim

Nature Angels

Earth Angels

Water Angels

Fire Angels

Air Angels

Healing Angels

Protection Angels

Guidance Angels

Karma Angels

Life Purpose Angels

Abundance Angels

Romance Angels

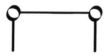

Family Angels

Animal Angels

Crystals Angels

Plants Angels

Sun Angels

Moon Angels

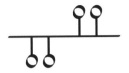

Knowledge & Wisdom Angels

Enlightenment &
Ascension Angels

Music Angels

Arts Angels

Sciences Angels

Transmutation Angels

Colors Angels

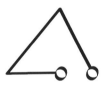

Symbols Angels

Stars Angels

Insight Angels

Laughter & Play Angels   Happiness Angels

Holy Spirit Angels

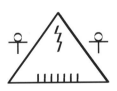

Christ Angels

Logos Angels

Holy Mother,
Divine Mother Angels

Yin/Yang Angels

White Light Angels

Golden Light Angels

Violet Light / Flame Angels

First Ray Angels

Second Ray Angels

Third Ray Angels

Fourth Ray Angels

Fifth Ray Angels

Sixth Ray Angels

Seventh Ray Angels

Eighth Ray Angels

Ninth Ray Angels

Tenth Ray Angels

Eleventh Ray Angels

Twelfth Ray Angels

Unknown Transcendental
Angels, Group A

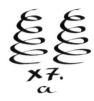

Transcendental
Superlight Angels

Unknown Angels of the Source,
Group B

Nirvana Angels, Group C

Ninth Dimension Angels,
Eloha Angels

Eighth Dimension Angels

Multidimensional Angels

Seventh Dimension Angels

Fifth Dimension Angels

Sixth Dimension Angels

Tenth Dimension Angels

Eleventh Dimension Angels

Twelfth Dimension Angels

Sirius Angels

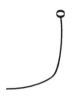

Pleiades Angels   Shamballa Angels   Dominion of Light   Unconditional Love

Blessings

Abadie, Marre Jeanne. *The Everything Guide to Angels.* MA: Adams Media, 2001.

Atteshlis, Stylianos. *The Esoteric Practice.* Cyprus: The Stoa Series, 1994.
The Esoteric Teachings. Cyprus: The Stoa Series, 1992.
Joshua Immanuel the Christ. Cyprus: The Stoa Series, 2001.
The Parables. Cyprus: The Stoa Series, 1991.
The Symbol of Life. Cyprus: The Stoa Series, 1998.
Words of Truth. Cyprus: The Stoa Series, 2009.

Briggs, Constance Victoria. *The Encyclopedia of Angels.* NY: Plume, 1997.

Bunson, Matthew. *Angels A to Z.* NY: Three Rivers Press, 1996.

Cooper, Diana. A Little Light on the Spiritual Laws. UK: Findhorn Press, 2007.
A New Light on Angels. UK: Findhorn Press, 2009.
A New Light on Ascension. UK: Findhorn Press, 2004.
Angel Answers. UK: Findhorn Press, 2007.
Angel Inspiration. UK: Findhorn Press, 2007.

Cortens, Theolyn. *Working with Archangels.* UK: Piaktus Books, Ltd., 2007.

Courtenay, Edwin. *The Archangelic Book of Ritual and Prayer.* Germany: The Prince of the Stars, 2006.

Cresswell, Julia. *The Watkins Dictionary of Angels.* London: Watkins Publishing, 2006.

Davidson, Gustav. *A Dictionary of Angels.* NY: The Free Press, 1967.

Giuley, Rosemary Ellen. *The Encyclopedia of Angels.* NY: Checkmark Books, 2004.

Gregg, Susan. *The Encyclopedia of Angels, Spirit Guides, and Ascended Masters.* USA: Fair Winds Press, 2008.

Paolino, Karen. *The Everything Guide to Angels.* MA: Adams Media, 2009.

Prophet, Elizabeth Clare. *How to Work with Angels.* USA: Summit University Press, 1998.
I Am Your Guard. USA: Summit University Press, 2008.
Violet Flame. USA: Summit University Press, 1998.

Raven, Hazel. *The Angel Bible.* London: Godsfield Press, Ltd., 2006.
The Angel Experience. London: Octopus Publishing, 2010.

Theotoki-Atteshli, Panayiota. *Gates to the Light.* Cyprus: The Stoa Series, 1996.

Virtue, Doreen. *Angels 101*. Carlsbad, CA: Hay House, 2006.
Angel Medicine. London: Hay House, 2004.
Angel Therapy. Carlsbad, CA: Hay House, 1997.
Angel Visions. Carlsbad, CA: Hay House, 2006.
Archangels 101. Carlsbad, CA: Hay House, 2010.
Archangels & Ascended Masters. Carlsbad, CA: Hay House, 2004.
Daily Guidance From Your Angels. Carlsbad, CA: Hay House, 2008.
Earth Angels. Carlsbad, CA: Hay House, 2008.
Goddesses and Angels. Carlsbad, CA: Hay House, 2006.
How to Hear Your Angels. Carlsbad, CA: Hay House, 2007.
Healing With The Angels. Carlsbad, CA: Hay House, 1999.
Messages From Your Angels. Carlsbad, CA: Hay House, 2002.
Realms of the Earth Angels. Carlsbad, CA: Hay House, 2007.
The Miracles of Archangel Michael. Carlsbad, CA: Hay House, 2009.
The Healing Miracles of Archangel Raphael. Carlsbad, CA: Hay House, 2010.

Virtue, Doreen and Charles Virtue. *Signs From Above*. Carlsbad, CA: Hay House, 2009.
Angel Words. Carlsbad, CA: Hay House, 2010.

Webster, Richard. Gabriel: *Communicating with the Archangel for Inspiration & Reconciliation*. USA: Llewellyn Publications, 2005.
Michael: Communicating with the Archangel for Guidance & Protection. USA: Llewellyn Publications, 2004.
Raphael: Communicating with the Archangel for Healing & Creativity. USA: Llewellyn Publications, 2005.
Spirit Guides & Angel Guardians. USA: Llewellyn Publications, 2004.
Uriel: Communicating with the Archangel for Transformation & Tranquility. USA: Llewellyn Publications, 2002.
The Encyclopedia of Angels. USA: Llewellyn Publications, 2009.

Also by Georgios Mylonas (Geom!*)

Angelic Invocations
Angelic Symbols
Angelic Meditations & Mysticism
The Golden Codes of Shamballa